# Middos, Manners & Morals
## With a Twist of Humor

### Joe Bobker

# About the Author

JOE BOBKER was born in 1947 in Ulm, a displaced persons' camp in Germany, to Polish Holocaust survivors Chaskel, *zt"l*, and Ida Bobker. On May 21, 1949, the family arrived in Sydney, Australia, on board the *Luciano Marnaro* liner as refugees from Adolf Hitler's reign of terror. The most searing influences on his Jewishness were his parents, two simple Yidden who saw over a hundred family members turned into ashes by the genocidal Nazi war machine, yet never swayed from their beliefs. Their faith was clearer than vision.

Bobker studied at the renowned Mercaz HaRav Kook Yeshiva in Kiryat Moshe, Jerusalem. Over the years he has been a popular speaker and became well known for dozens of articles concerning Jews and Judaism in the one hundred-year-old *Los Angeles Jewish Times*, where he was publisher and editor in chief.

A prolific and creative writer, his books cover a variety of Jewish subjects emerging from an intimate yet philosophical, erudite and witty perspective.

Since 1980, Bobker has lived in both Los Angeles and New York with his wife Miriam, a barrister from Melbourne, Australia, also the child of Polish Holocaust survivors.

When asked where he gets his inspiration, Joe replied, "Eli, Avi, Benny, Dovi, Hadassa, Baylie, Layella, Devorah, Dalia, Toby, Chesky, Yoni, Baruch, Zevi, Mattie, Mordechai, Henny, Dovid, Shira, Asher, Gali, Daniel and Leah — my four sons, four daughters-in-law, granddaughters and grandsons (as of Shavuos 2008)."

# Other Books by the Author

*Torah with a Twist of Humor*

*And You Thought There Were Only Four! 400 Questions to Make Your Seder More Enlightening, Educational and Enjoyable!*

*From Fasting to Feasting: A Unique Journey through the Jewish Holidays*

*Torah News U Can Use: I Didn't Know That!*

*Pirkei Avos with a Twist of Humor*

*Can I Play Chess on Shabbas?*

*Shalom Bayis with a Twist of Humor*

# MIDDOS, MANNERS & M⦿RALS...

## WITH A TWIST OF HUMOR

### FIFTY-TWO WEEKLY TIPS AND DOZENS OF ANECDOTES FROM THE SAGES OF ISRAEL

# JOE BOBKER

JERUSALEM ♦ NEW YORK

Copyright © Joe Bobker
Jerusalem 2009/5769

All rights reserved. No part of this publication may be translated, reproduced, stored in a retrieval system or transmitted, in any form or by any means, electronic, mechanical, photocopying, recording or otherwise, without express written permission from the publishers.

Layout: Marzel A.S. — Jerusalem
Cover design: S. Kim Glassman
Cover Art: Avi Katz

ISBN: 978-965-229-448-7
Edition   1 3 5 7 9 8 6 4 2

Gefen Publishing House Ltd.
6 Hatzvi St.
Jerusalem 94386, Israel
972-2-538-0247
orders@gefenpublishing.com

Gefen Books
600 Broadway
Lynbrook, NY 11563, USA
1-516-593-1234
orders@gefenpublishing.com

www.israelbooks.com

Printed in Israel

*Send for our free catalogue*

# Contents

About the Author & Other Books by the Author . . . . . . . . . . . . . . . . . . . . . ii
Acknowledgments . . . . . . . . . . . . . . . . . . . . . . . . . . . . . . . . . . . . . . . . . . ix
Caveat . . . . . . . . . . . . . . . . . . . . . . . . . . . . . . . . . . . . . . . . . . . . . . . . . . . xi
Introduction . . . . . . . . . . . . . . . . . . . . . . . . . . . . . . . . . . . . . . . . . . . . . . xv

**Week 1**    On *Ahavas Yisroel* . . . . . . . . . . . . . . . . . . . . . . . . . . . . . 1
               The Golden Rule: First, Do No Harm!

**Week 2**    On Aliya . . . . . . . . . . . . . . . . . . . . . . . . . . . . . . . . . . . . . 7
               Eretz Yisroel: Beloved, More Than Anything Else!

**Week 3**    On Anger, Bearing Grudges . . . . . . . . . . . . . . . . . . . . . . 13
               Spare the Rod

**Week 4**    On Avoiding Evil People . . . . . . . . . . . . . . . . . . . . . . . . 19
               Pick Your Friends Carefully!

**Week 5**    On Being Concerned for Others . . . . . . . . . . . . . . . . . . 25
               My Chumra's Better Than Your Chumra!

**Week 6**    On Being Content . . . . . . . . . . . . . . . . . . . . . . . . . . . . 31
               Peace of Mind

**Week 7**    On *Bikur Cholim* . . . . . . . . . . . . . . . . . . . . . . . . . . . . . 37
               The Infinite Mitzva

**Week 8**    On Borrowing Money . . . . . . . . . . . . . . . . . . . . . . . . . . 43
               Borrow to Banquet!

**Week 9**    On Bribery, Justice . . . . . . . . . . . . . . . . . . . . . . . . . . . . 49
               Law and Disorder

**Week 10**   On *Chesed shel Emes*, Eulogies . . . . . . . . . . . . . . . . . . . 55
               The Most *Bona Fide* Mitzva of Them All

**Week 11**   On Clarity in Teaching Torah . . . . . . . . . . . . . . . . . . . . 61
               What? Say That Again?

**Week 12** On Commerce — Wages and Prices . . . . . . . . . . . . . . . . 67
A Hard Day's Night

**Week 13** On Conflict, Controversy . . . . . . . . . . . . . . . . . . . . . . 73
Time Out!

**Week 14** On *Da'as Torah* . . . . . . . . . . . . . . . . . . . . . . . . . . . . 79
When Right Is Left

**Week 15** On *Derech Eretz,* Respect . . . . . . . . . . . . . . . . . . . . . 85
What's Yours Is Mine!

**Week 16** On Doing What's Right — Free Will . . . . . . . . . . . . . . 91
Doing What Comes Naturally!

**Week 17** On Flattery — The "Evil Eye" . . . . . . . . . . . . . . . . . . . 97
Flattery Will Get You…Nowhere?

**Week 18** On Fleeing Falsehood — *Emes* . . . . . . . . . . . . . . . . . 103
Liar, Liar!

**Week 19** On Forgiveness . . . . . . . . . . . . . . . . . . . . . . . . . . . . 109
To Forgive Is to Be Forgiven

**Week 20** On *Gemilus Chasadim* . . . . . . . . . . . . . . . . . . . . . . 115
Good Deeds Are Better Than Wise Sayings

**Week 21** On *Giving the Benefit of the Doubt* . . . . . . . . . . . . . . 121
Seeing Is Not Believing!

**Week 22** Gone Fishing! . . . . . . . . . . . . . . . . . . . . . . . . . . . . . 127

**Week 23** On Greeting with a Smile . . . . . . . . . . . . . . . . . . . . . 131
Smile…and the World Smiles with You!

**Week 24** On *Hachnasas Kalla,* Sharing in *Simchas* . . . . . . . . . . 137
*Simcha* Blues

**Week 25** On *Hachnasas Orchim* . . . . . . . . . . . . . . . . . . . . . . 143
It's Not Enough to Just Open the Door!

**Week 26** On Harming Another — Friends and Enemies . . . . . . . . 149
With a Little Help from My Friends

**Week 27**  On Honoring Parents . . . . . . . . . . . . . . . . . . . . . . . . . . 155
Parents? Partners in Creation!

**Week 28**  On Jealousy, Coveting . . . . . . . . . . . . . . . . . . . . . . . . 161
Invite It Not!

**Week 29**  On Leadership, Fundraising . . . . . . . . . . . . . . . . . . . . 167
Appearances Matter

**Week 30**  On *Loshen Hora*, Slander . . . . . . . . . . . . . . . . . . . . . . 173
Watch Your Tongue!

**Week 31**  On *Ma'aser* . . . . . . . . . . . . . . . . . . . . . . . . . . . . . . . . . 179
The Ten Percent Rule

**Week 32**  On Making Money, Honesty in Business . . . . . . . . . . . . 185
Even Chanoch Was a Cobbler!

**Week 33**  On Making Peace . . . . . . . . . . . . . . . . . . . . . . . . . . . . 191
Pots and Peace

**Week 34**  On *Midda k'Neged Midda* . . . . . . . . . . . . . . . . . . . . . . 197
What Goes 'Round, Comes 'Round!

**Week 35**  On Modesty, Humility, Pride . . . . . . . . . . . . . . . . . . . 203
What Came First? The Gnat or Man?

**Week 36**  On Patience, Persistence . . . . . . . . . . . . . . . . . . . . . . 209
Sounds of Silence

**Week 37**  On Prayer . . . . . . . . . . . . . . . . . . . . . . . . . . . . . . . . . 215
From Your Mouth to God's Ear!

**Week 38**  On Rebuke, Offering Advice . . . . . . . . . . . . . . . . . . . . 221
The *Tzadik* in Peltz

**Week 39**  On Respecting Elders, Honoring *Talmidei Chachamim* . . . . . . 227
The "Wings of Israel"

**Week 40**  On Selfishness, Sensitivity . . . . . . . . . . . . . . . . . . . . . 233
Sensitive to Sensitivity

**Week 41**  On *Shalom Bayis* . . . . . . . . . . . . . . . . . . . . . . . . 239
For Domestic Bliss Do All the Don'ts!

**Week 42**  On Shame . . . . . . . . . . . . . . . . . . . . . . . . . . . . . . 245
The Name of the Game Is Shame

**Week 43**  On Showing Gratitude, *Hakoras Hatov* . . . . . . . . . . . . . . . 251
Saying Thanks!

**Week 44**  On Stealing, Returning, Using Lost Objects . . . . . . . . . . . . 257
A Thief Is a Thief Is a Thief…

**Week 45**  On Supporting Torah Scholars and Institutions . . . . . . . . . 263
Rejoice, Zevulun!

**Week 46**  On Taking Advantage of Another Person . . . . . . . . . . . . 269
Stepping on Toes

**Week 47**  On Teaching Torah to Others . . . . . . . . . . . . . . . . . . . 275
The Joy of Torah Is Torah

**Week 48**  On Time Management . . . . . . . . . . . . . . . . . . . . . . . 281
Well, It's about Time!

**Week 49**  On Torah as a Protective Umbrella . . . . . . . . . . . . . . . . 287
And Students Are Its Towers!

**Week 50**  On *Tzedaka* . . . . . . . . . . . . . . . . . . . . . . . . . . . . . 293
If You Give, You Get!

**Week 51**  On Work . . . . . . . . . . . . . . . . . . . . . . . . . . . . . . . . 299
My Son, the Thief!

**Week 52**  On Zealousness . . . . . . . . . . . . . . . . . . . . . . . . . . . 305
Rush Hour

Afterword . . . . . . . . . . . . . . . . . . . . . . . . . . . . . . . . . . . . . . 311
General Endnotes for Further Study . . . . . . . . . . . . . . . . . . . . . 313
Joe Bobker Collection of Books . . . . . . . . . . . . . . . . . . . . . . . 320

# Acknowledgments

I would like to thank my mentor and teacher, HaRav Osher Abramson, *zt"l*, a Holocaust survivor, and my wife Miriam, epitome of *middos* and exemplifier of good manners, who has given new meaning to the words *patience* and *understanding*. Without her support and serenity this book — like all those that have preceded it — would still be on my shelf instead of yours.

# Caveat

This book is not a halachic guide, nor a source of halachic rulings. It is a book on motivation and inspiration. Its sole purpose is to open the curtain slightly on the subject of *mussar* (manners) and, hopefully, entice the reader to learn more about Jewish ethics. The endnotes may not be entirely accurate, but will put the reader on the right path for further study. If you have specific questions, consult a qualified rabbi.

"We're forever meeting people who have watches,
very seldom people who have compasses.

We always need to know what time it is, but we never
ask ourselves where we are, or where we're heading!"

— *Georges Perec*

# Introduction

*"Kodem a mensch — un nach dem heilig!*
*(First be a mensch — then be holy!)"*

— Kotzker Rebbe

In the days of the Temple, Jews would perform the ritual known as *"bensching lulav"* on each day of the festival of Succos, including Shabbas. To avoid carrying on Shabbas, a prohibited act, they would bring their *lulavim* to the Temple *erev Shabbas* and leave them there. Because it would have been impossible to find one's own personal *lulav* in all the piles of *lulavim*, each Jew declared that it was OK if someone else used his *lulav*, which would then be considered a gift.

When the people came back Shabbas morning the Temple workers would hand out the piles of *lulavim* to the crowd, but each year a small riot broke out as Jews shoved and pushed each other trying to get the best-looking *lulav*.

How did the rabbis respond? Faced with a choice between complying with a specific mitzva ordered by the Torah (*bensching lulav*) or countenancing violence amongst Jews, the rabbis chose to ban the mitzva for the sake of peaceful conduct (*menschlichkeit*).

*Lech lecha*, God tells Avraham.

Most scholars translate this as "Get up and go!" But not the *Zohar*.

Kabbala's interpretation of God's instruction is more psychological: "Go to yourself!" In other words, Avraham is not to become just a geographic vagabond, but a seeker of a new identity, on a search for himself, an inward spiritual odyssey.

This journey requires a backpack filled with manners and morals, known in Torah shorthand as *middos*.

The lesson in the *Lech Lecha* expression is this: spiritual maturity requires movement. The first step towards improvement is just that…a step! Apathy is the enemy of *middos*; staying put is a recipe for failure.

The Steipler Rav used to urge *rabbeim* to "spice up" their teachings with short anecdotes and lessons that inspire *yiras Shamayim*.

The anecdotes and lessons outlined in this *middos* book are intended to act as a collective tuning fork to help one adjust to the music of a Jewish life. *Middos* are a compass for our exploration toward becoming a better Jew, a state of mind that requires not just learning, but *being*.

Remember: "What we do is more important than what we study," teaches Rabbi Yehuda Hanasi, compiler of the Talmud, to which Rabbi Meir adds, "It's not what you know how to do, but what you have the character to do!"

The Alter of Kelm couldn't tolerate bad manners, so every student sent to his yeshiva was given one *midda* to perfect whilst they were learning there. One boy spent seven years just on *savlanus* (patience). Rav Aaron Kotler urged his students to infuse new meanings into old habits. Meanwhile, Yisroel Salanter thought it more difficult to change one bad character trait (e.g., anger, laziness, etc.) than to learn all of Shas. The founder of the *mussar* movement recalls:

> When I began to study *mussar* I became upset at the world at large. However, as for myself, I thought I was faultless. As time progressed, I soon realized that I had many faults of my own. I thus became upset at myself too. I reached a point where I judged everyone else favorably. I then began to look down at no one's deeds but my own.

The final word goes to Reb Menachem Mendel of Kotzk. Commenting on the Torah verse "*V'anshei kodesh te'heyu li* (And ye shall be holy men unto Me)," the Kotzker Rebbe added, "*Kodem a mensch — un nach dem heilig* (First be a *mensch* — then be holy)!"

Joe Bobker

Rosh Hashana 2008

# Week 1

## On *Ahavas Yisroel*

The loneliest person is someone who loves only himself!
— *Yiddish folk saying*

A poor man once entered the *beis medrash* of Rav Tzvi Neviasky and asked if he could address the *shul*, explain his circumstances, and perhaps receive some *tzedaka*. Rav Tzvi declined on the basis that it would interfere with his scheduled Gemora *shiur*.

Rav Yisroel Salanter overheard this exchange and turned to Rav Tzvi, asking, "Have you ever wondered why Hillel interprets the *pasuk* 'Love your fellow as yourself' to mean, 'What you dislike, do not do unto others'? Why use the negative form as opposed to saying, 'Do for others what you would like for yourself'? The answer is that sometimes what one person likes comes at the expense of another. For example, you would like to have your *shiur* in Gemora, but this would be to the disadvantage of the hungry *darshan*. This is why Hillel expressed this important principle in the negative form. Rather than impose the *shiur* on the guest simply because that is what you want, consider the fact that you would not like someone to harm you even if it were to be to someone else's advantage. This approach is the more encompassing and safer one, for one simply cannot go wrong by refraining from doing something to others that he himself would not like, but may stumble in the mitzva of loving his fellow Jew by imposing on him something that he himself likes. Therefore, do not hurt your fellow Jew just because you want to have your *shiur*!"

# The Golden Rule: First, Do No Harm!

> A student once complained to Rav Meir that during Elul he was unable to learn properly because he was too busy helping new students get settled in. Rav Meir replied, "Although learning Torah is the most important mitzva there are times when others need you. Giving is what one must do. You ought to view this not as closing your own Gemora but as opening many more Gemoras for your new friends!"

Rabbi Akiva considered his Golden Rule, *V'ahavta l'reiacha k'mocha* (usually translated "love your friend as yourself") to mean "love every single Jew as *he* loves himself," which the Rambam codifies as a commandment, as *the* fundamental essence of the Torah.

The full verse includes a reason ("I am God"), which acts as a reminder: since man was created "in My image," hating another Jew is hating both *yourself* and God. And so Reb Levi Yitzchak of Berdichev concluded, "Whether one truly loves God can be determined by the love he shows to his fellow men!"

The famous Hillel response ("What is hateful to you do not do to others!") to a non-Jew's teach-me-the-entire-Torah-while-I-stand-on-one-foot demand was brilliant. Why? Because Hillel realized that loving another was too difficult to do "right off the bat" — as a Sholem Aleichem character once sighed, "As a rule, people love another from a distance!" — so Hillel reversed it from the positive ("love your fellow Jew") to the negative: first, do no harm!

> "If one loves a *talmid chacham*, that is not *ahavas Yisroel*," Rav Avraham Yehoshua Heschel, the Kapishnitzer Rebbe, used to say, "that is *ahavas Torah*. To love a rich person is not *ahavas Yisroel*, it is a love of money. To love a Jew who is neither a *talmid chacham* nor a wealthy person, now that is *ahavas Yisroel*!"

*Hevei nosei v'nosein* (be a carrier and a giver) is an odd Talmud expression; it can also mean, "Let's do a deal!"

For example, if you were a car dealer you would be *hevei nosei v'nosein* in cars; if you were a furniture store, you would be *hevei nosei v'nosein* in furniture, and so on.

When applying this expression to interpersonal relationships (*bein adam l'chaveiro*), the Talmud is relying on the "profit" factor. If you motivate yourself as if chasing a business transaction, the same inspiration and ambition give you a higher chance of success in giving!

> Rav Nosson Wachtfogel was asked if there was any difference between *chesed* (kindness) and *nosei b'ol chaveiro* (bearing your fellow's burden), two traits that always seem to overlap. The difference, the *rav* explained, is that *chesed* is an act of one person, in contrast to *nosei b'ol chaveiro* which merges the "giver and getter" into *one* person (i.e., his problem is my problem; his *simcha* is my *simcha*, etc.).

There is a tendency in the English translation of *V'ahavta l'reiacha k'mocha* to leave one word out (*l'*, "to"), giving us instead, "Love your fellow Jew as yourself." But the word "to" is important: it's a twin reminder that caring must be directed "to" *someone* in particular, and you as the giver must be sensitive to give what the recipient actually needs, not what you think he or she might need.

In explaining the presence of this important word, Rabbeinu Tam makes reference to the difference between the *al* (e.g., *al netilas yadayim*) and the *l'* (e.g., *l'hadlik ner shel Chanuka*) in certain blessings.

The *al* appears in the context of an imminent mitzva (e.g., washing hands), whereas the *l'* applies to mitzvos that extend into the future (e.g., lighting Chanuka candles tomorrow). Thus the presence of *l'*, within the context of loving another, is an obligation that requires follow-through; it might start now but finishes only later, lasting forever, throughout life.

> One day Rav Baruch Ber Leibowitz, the *rosh yeshiva* of Kaminetz, failed to show up to an important meeting. One of his students was sent to his home to check up and when he arrived there, he was shocked to see Rav Baruch Ber standing at the door in his bare feet.
>
> "What happened?" the boy asked.
>
> "A poor man knocked on my door earlier," the *rosh yeshiva* explained, "and I noticed that his shoes were completely worn out. So I gave him mine. They were my only pair."

Rav Eliyahu Dessler's tip, "To love another Jew, do so actively and givingly (*hevei nosei v'nosein*)," was based on his conviction that the more unconditional giving you do *consciously*, the more the loving comes naturally.

Remember: the Hebrew word for love is *ahava*, a combination of *ani* and *hav*, which means "I give."

Mrs. Spiegel is called to serve on a jury and asks to be excused.

"Why?" asks the judge.

"Because I don't believe in capital punishment and I don't want my personal beliefs to prevent me from making the right decision."

The judge is impressed with her thoughtfulness and tells her, "Ma'am, this is not a murder trial but a simple civil lawsuit. A wife is bringing a case against her husband because he recklessly gambled away the $35,000 he had promised to use to remodel her kitchen for her birthday."

"Oh, in that case," Mrs. Spiegel says, "I'll definitely serve. In fact, I could be wrong about capital punishment after all!"

# Week 2

## On Aliya

The journey of a thousand miles begins with a single "oy"!
— *Yiddish folk saying*

A young man studying in Rav Noach Weinberg's Aish HaTorah yeshiva in Jerusalem once decided to leave and search for some spiritual meaning. For two weeks he wandered in and out of *shuls* in Meah Shearim and visited the graves of *tzadikim* throughout Eretz Yisroel. He then returned to the yeshiva and complained to Rav Noach that he had searched and searched yet found "absolutely nothing!"

Rav Noach patiently asked him whether, during his trek across the Holy Land, he had found any baffoo sticks.

"Baffoo sticks?" asked the confused student, "I have no idea what a baffoo stick is."

"And," asked Rav Noach, "you *know* what spirituality is?"

# Eretz Yisroel: Beloved, More Than Anything Else!

> On one of his many fundraising trips to South Africa, the Klausenberger Rebbe met a man who was disappointed after his recent trip to Eretz Yisroel, complaining, "I was in several different places and witnessed such awful desecration of our holy Shabbas!"
>
> "That's odd!" replied the Rebbe, "I've been living in Eretz Yisroel for many years now, and I've never seen the places that you mention. You, on the other hand, were there for only a few days and you managed to find so many faults!"
>
> The Klausenberger Rebbe pinpointed human nature: if you approach something with a negative attitude, you'll always find something wrong; on the other hand, if you want to see good qualities and not just faults, you'll only see the good in the world.

Throughout Jewish history, thousands of Jews have yearned to visit and experience the *kedusha* of what the Vilna Gaon described as "the precious Holy Land"!

The early *Tanna'im* kissed its holy stones on arrival, some even rolling in its earth, "cherishing her stones and favoring her dust."

When Avraham and Moshe wanted to get a good look at Israel, God told them "*Sa na einecha u're'eh* (Lift up your eyes and see)." Why? At eye level, it looks like any other country. But if you look closely, you'll see, and feel, a holiness that no other land possesses.

In fact, God waited until Avraham entered Eretz Yisroel before entering into His Covenant.

When the *meraglim* tried to justify their slander of Israel by saying, "We are not speaking of the Land *per se*," it didn't help them. God recognized defamation and gross disrespect when He saw it, and reacted accordingly.

*Einei Hashem Elokecha ba*, "God's attention is constantly on it (the holy land of Eretz Yisroel)!"

> Rav Eliyahu Dessler was reaching old age when Rav Yosef Shlomo Kahanamen invited him to move to B'nei Brak and serve as *mashgiach* in the Ponivezh Yeshiva. Rav Dessler was there for just a short time when he started speaking enthusiastically about his impressions of Eretz Yisroel. His cousin, Rav Shlomo Zalman Dessler, asked how he could form such a quick opinion without touring the country, or at least the city! "In just two hours,"

Rav Eliyahu replied, "I've already attained levels of spirituality that take weeks to reach in *chutz la'aretz*!"

Since "Eretz Yisroel is beloved by Me [God] *more than anything else*," *Pirkei d'Rabbi Eliezer* gushes that its very air makes you wise, that "even the local shepherds are worthier than all the wise men outside of it!"

A Torah scholar who leaves Israel, warns Shimon ben Eleazar, "diminishes in worth!" The poet of Israel, Yehuda Halevi, sings, "Nothing can be perfect, except in Israel!"

The rabbis of the Talmud elevate the mitzva of dwelling in the Holy Land as being "equal to all other mitzvos combined!"

And so, a full century *before* Herzl's *The Jewish State* appeared, dozens of pious Jews were going on aliya, encouraged by Rabbi Naftali Zvi Yehuda Berlin (the Netziv), the Vilna Gaon lobbied aggressively for aliya (whilst a *meshugene* wealthy Jew in the United States, Mordecai Noah, was appealing to European Jewry to go on "aliya" to the Grand Island of the Niagara River!), and, *erev* Tisha b'Av, the *Chasam Sofer* gave a *d'var Torah* urging all diaspora Jews, "Go now!"

> In 1916, the Gerer Rebbe, Rav Avraham Mordechai Alter, expressed his wish to visit Eretz Yisroel, but his brother-in-law, Rav Chanoch Tzvi of Bendin, tried to discourage him. "What if you arrive in the Holy Land and meet unworthy community leaders? Then, when you return to Poland, you will feel the need to warn us about them and then you will have besmirched Hashem's beloved country. What do you need that for?"
>
> "You needn't worry," replied the Rebbe. "I will make sure to see and hear only good things!"

Rabbi Yosef Chaim Sonnenfeld would often quote the Tehillim verse "Gaze upon the goodness of Yerushalayim" as a reminder to only focus on the positive aspects of the holy city.

When Rav Yisroel Zev Gustman decided to go on aliya, in 1961, he chose to go by boat rather than by plane, so he could have time to prepare himself spiritually for the Holy Land.

When one of his pupils asked him whether he should move to Eretz Yisroel, the *Chazon Ish* replied, "If only you had told me that you had already decided to move, you would have doubled my joy!"

An elderly Jewish couple from New York are touring Israel by car. One cold winter day whilst driving in the northern Galilee it starts to pour. The sleet builds up on the windows and the wiper blades are not working properly. Unable to see, the husband gets out and starts overturning large boulders and rocks on the side of the road. His wife thinks he's gone crazy. Suddenly, he discovers two lethargic hibernating rattle snakes, grabs them, straightens them out flat and installs them on his window blades.

"What?! Are you totally meshuge?" his wife screams at him.

"No," he calmly replies. "Haven't you ever heard of vind chilled vipers?"

# Week 3

## On Anger, Bearing Grudges

*If you can't bite, don't show your teeth.*
— *Yiddish folk saying*

When Rav Shlomo Zalman Auerbach was told that one of his *talmidim* was living in a Sha'arei Chesed apartment where the two landlords were fighting, he told him, "Leave the apartment immediately!"

A week later Rav Shlomo Zalman asked him, "*Nu*, have you moved apartments yet? It is forbidden to remain there! Here is a list of apartments that I have found to be available!"

At that point the student realized that Rav Shlomo Zalman was totally serious about his moving out of the apartment, so he moved, in order to run far away from an argument — even if it wasn't his!

# Spare the Rod

> The assistant to the Chozeh (Seer) of Lublin once forgot to prepare a *netilas yadayim* cup beside his rebbe's bed. When the Chozeh awoke, he found no water and was ready to accuse his assistant of negligence. However, just as the assistant entered the room, the Chozeh remembered Chazal's (our Sages') admonition: "One who gets angry is considered as though he worshipped idols." The Chozeh took a moment to consider: is *avoda zara* (idol worship) any better than not washing *netilas yadayim*?

Anger is the most dangerous of emotions, especially inappropriate in parents or leaders. Look what happened to Moshe and the rock! One tap and he was forbidden from entering the Promised Land!

"When a wise person becomes angry, his wisdom flees from him; when a prophet becomes angry, his prophecy flees from him!"

An angry man?

Worse than an idol worshipper, says the Rambam. Don't even get angry on "heavenly matters," writes Rav Yosef Caro, whilst Yonatan ben Eleazar was convinced that "the road to hell [is opened] by the gates of anger!"

The Brisker Rav would tolerate a person giving one disciplinary smack to a child, but not two. The second, he was convinced, was done more out of anger than rebuke. When the shepherds of Gerar started up with Yitzchak he simply walked away rather than lose his temper, thus earning the reputation of being *ma'avir al midosav*, one who "rises above his characteristics," repaying hatred with love.

The rabbis of the Talmud praise "those who are insulted but not affected, who experience shame but do not respond." *Meiri* was convinced that when a person becomes angry he harms himself, physically, emotionally, spiritually.

"The beginning of a quarrel is like releasing water!" If a leak (i.e., a potential argument) is not sealed right away, the Talmud warns, it will grow and ultimately be impossible to fix.

> Rav Moshe Feinstein had a calm and easygoing disposition and never lost his temper even during stressful times and aggravating situations. He once confided to his *talmidim*, "Do you think that this is my natural instinct? On the contrary, by nature I am short tempered, but I make a great effort to overcome my instincts."

And so the siddur's *Amida tefilla* pleads, "To those who curse me, let my soul be silent!"

Anger is seen as a tragic state of mind which leads to a catastrophic loss of self-control.

Rabbeinu Tam describes anger as one of the worst character traits: "An angry person does not realize what he is doing…; he may transgress some of the most severe *aveiros*…. One cannot expect to succeed in *avodas Hashem* unless he can control his anger."

Rav Yehuda Hachassid once told a parent to pay his children's rebbe whatever he owed him and then get another teacher quickly. When asked why, he said he saw him lose his temper at the boy.

Before moving to *Eretz Yisroel*, Rav Aron Hakohen was warned by his father-in-law, the *Chofetz Chaim*, not to sleep a single night in any city that was ridden with controversy.

Avoiding conflict was a recurrent theme throughout the letters of the *Chazon Ish*: "Peace is what I love…. The smallest grain of *machlokes*, even seemingly as insignificant as wind-blown chaffe, burdens me like the heavy beams of an olive press…. I am not accustomed to becoming entangled in disputes…; there is where the Satan dances and tries to create hatred and discord!"

> In a letter to his son studying in the Mirrer Yeshiva, Rav Tzvi Pesach Frank wrote: "Our living Torah teaches us to be pleasant in our ways, to forgo our rights and overlook any insult to our honor. You should also realize that disputes and grudges are a source of *bitul Torah*, *loshen hora* and a distraction from one's *tefillos*. It is your holy obligation to stay very far away from these types of sentiments!"

"Anger lingers only in the chest of fools," insisted King Solomon.

"I don't believe there is ever good reason to be angry," Rav Shach once advised a man who was enraged at another, "and I'll tell you why. If a person were to do some introspection, he would realize that he is guilty of the exact same things for which he blames his friend. In that case, how can his complaints be justified?"

Rabbi Tzvi Hirsch Zacks recalls that on several occasions his grandfather Rabbi Yisroel Meir Hakohen, the *Chofetz Chaim*, would enter the *beis medrash* at midnight, open the *aron kodesh* and cry, "*Ribono shel Olam*, I, Yisroel Meir, am a *kohen* and therefore prone to becoming angry. Please, *Hashem*, assist me so that I will be able to overcome such feelings!"

Young Surele is doing her English homework and asks her father, "Tati, what's the difference between anger and exasperation?"

"It's a matter of degree," he replies. "Let me show you what I mean."

The father then picks up the phone and dials a number at random. When a voice answers he says, "Hi! Is Joe there?"

"No," the man camly answers, "there's no one here by that name."

"See," the father explains to his daughter. "He was not happy with our call but was OK with it. Now watch."

The father dials again. "Hello, is Joe there?"

"Now look here! You just called this number and I told you that there is no Joe here! You've got a lot of nerve calling again!" The receiver gets slammed down hard.

"You see," the father explains, "that was anger. Now I'll show you what exasperation means."

He dials the number again, and when a violent voice answers, he calmly says, "Hi! This is Joe. Any calls for me?"

# Week 4

## On Avoiding Evil People

When a crook kisses you, count your teeth!
— *Yiddish folk saying*

An old man sat outside the walls of a great city. When travelers approached they would ask the old man, "What kind of people live in this city?" and the old man would answer, "What kind of people lived in the place you came from?"

If the travelers answered, "Only bad people lived in the place where we have came from," then the old man would reply, "Continue on, you will only find bad people here."

But if the travelers answered, "Only good people lived in the place where we have come from," then the old man would say, "Enter, for here too, you will only find good people."

As the Yiddish saying goes, when you always drink vinegar you don't know anything sweeter exists!

# Pick Your Friends Carefully!

An irreligious Jew once moved into an apartment and got to know his neighbor, a righteous *talmid chacham*, who greeted him warmly and over time had a very positive influence on him. Slowly but surely, the man grew closer to Torah and started to keep mitzvos. But then another neighbor moved in who not only had no interest in Torah and mitzvos but was hostile to religion. Soon, the *talmid chacham* began to see all of his efforts go down the drain as the two became close friends and his new *chaver* began to return to his old ways. Not knowing what to do, he went to get advice.

"Surely you know that everything in this world was created for a purpose," said the *Chofetz Chaim*. "So for what purpose do you think *loshen hora* and *rechilus* were created? For situations such as these. If a heretic is having a negative influence on others, it is a mitzva to speak *loshen hora* about him. The details of his wickedness should be made public so that people will distance themselves from him!"

The man followed the advice, and it worked.

"The urge to evil enters as a guest," warns *Midrash Rabba*, "and soon becomes the host!"

There are three kinds of friends, according to the *Mivchar Hapeninim*: "One like food which one cannot do without; one like medicine which you may need now and then; and one like pestilence which no one needs at all!"

Have you ever noticed that whenever Avraham is with Lot, God never appears?

Rashi explains that the two could not coexist because of Lot's wicked nature, a lesson that Jews should avoid mixing with immoral people. Even if Lot wasn't evil, he was to be avoided because of his choice to associate with the evil folks of Sodom, knowing that they were "exceedingly wicked towards *Hashem*."

"A person of virtue among the wicked is better than a person of virtue among the righteous," notes *Sefer Chassidim*, "and a person who sins among the righteous is worse than a person who sins among the wicked!"

The Torah describes how the people of Ashur, in contrast to their children who joined Nimrod's rebellion against God, flourished once they separated themselves from the bad influences of their neighbors.

"One who follows the wise will become wise," writes King Solomon; "one who follows the fools will become evil." And surely it's no coincidence that hardheartedness (*immutz halev*), a prerequisite for evil, is the first of the forty-four specific sins in Yom Kippur's *Al Cheit*.

The lesson?

Choose your friends (*chaverim*, "associates") carefully; and, adds Rabbeinu Asher (*Rosh*), help choose your children's friends even more carefully!

"Acquire for yourself a friend," instructs the Mishna, adding, make sure it's "a good friend!" Meanwhile, the usually pessimistic *Koheles* suddenly becomes upbeat when it comes to friends ("Two are better than one!").

The fifth Rebbe of Chabad waxed poetic about the advantages of friendship; "When one meets a truly devoted friend, not only does he feel good and forget all his troubles, he even enjoys a newly awakened inner liveliness and optimism!"

"Friendship is like a stone," notes Chassidic Rebbe Mordechai of Lechovitz, "a stone has no value, but when you rub two stones together properly, sparks of fire emerge!"

> Rav Aryeh Levin was walking with his friend Rav Avraham Ganchovsky through Jerusalem when a poor Jerusalemite asked Rav Aryeh for money. He reached into his pocket but quickly realized that he had no money on him, so he turned to Rav Avraham and said, "Will you please lend me ten *lirot*?"
>
> "Why borrow? We're friends! Here, I'll give him some money."
>
> "No, no," said Rav Aryeh, "This is no time for friendship. A mitzva has come my way and I'm unwilling to pass up this opportunity!"

What's the definition of a "good" friend?

According to Rabbi Ovadia of Bartenura it's one who isn't afraid to give you constructive criticism.

In his ethical will, Asher ben Yechiel urges his children, "Never be weary of making friends; consider a single enemy as one too many. If you have a faithful friend, hold fast to him. Let him not go, for he is a precious possession!"

Several evil pirates walk into a bar and order drinks. The bartender notices that one has been roughed up bad, and asks him, "Hey, how did you get the wooden leg?"

"Well, we were in a battle and I got hit with a cannon ball, and I lost my leg."

"I'm sorry to hear that. But how did you also get a hook for your hand?"

"Well, we were in another battle. I boarded a ship and got into a sword fight. My hand was cut off. I got fitted with a hook."

"Wow, I'm sorry to hear that. But what about that eye patch?"

"Well, one day I was lying on the beach sun baking when a bird flew over and dropped something in my eye."

"Wait a minute! You don't lose your eye from that!"

"You do if it's your first day with the hook!"

# Week 5

## On Being Concerned for Others

*A man who is filled with himself has no room for God.*
— *Yiddish folk saying*

Rav Aryeh Leib, son of the *Chofetz Chaim*, recalled how one Pesach they were visiting his mother's uncle and were offered matza pancakes. The *Chofetz Chaim* did not eat *gebrochts*, matza that has come into contact with water; nevertheless he ate a few pancakes, later explaining that it was preferable to eat a minimal amount rather than make his host feel uncomfortable! So concerned was the *Chofetz Chaim* for others that when he davened *Ma'ariv* on *motzei* Yom Kippur as the *shaliach tzibbur*, he raced through it as fast as he could — so that the *kehilla* could get home and break their fast quicker!

As a young sixteen-year-old yeshiva *bochur*, Rav Yoel Klopt, future *av beis din* of Haifa, studied at the Radin Yeshiva. Rav Yoel recalls that early one morning he was learning in the *beis medrash* before *Shacharis* when the *Chofetz Chaim* entered the room. When the eighty-year-old *Chofetz Chaim* saw him he made a detour around the entire perimeter of the *beis medrash* to reach his place in order not to inconvenience a young student to rise in his honor.

# My Chumra's Better Than Your Chumra!

> Rav Yisroel Salanter was once a guest in a home at the top of a hill. When he washed for the meal, he only washed his fingers and not his entire hands (the traditional procedure). When asked why, he replied that the maid had to carry heavy buckets of water from a well up a hill to supply water to the house. The faster water was used up, the harder she had to work. He was washing in the minimal manner allowed by Torah law so that she would not have to suffer.

"When we die," notes the Talmud, "and appear to answer for our lives in Heaven, God will not ask, 'Did you believe in Me?' but 'How have you dealt with those around you?'"

Zealousness for Torah is nullified if it creates discomfort, irritation or inconvenience to others. Both Rav Dessler and Rav Yechezkel Abramsky were generally against new *chumros* ("additional stringencies") because they inevitably complicated matters *bein adam l'chaveiro*.

One *erev Shabbas* the *Alter* of Slabodka, Rav Nosson Tzvi Finkel, stopped a student who made it a point of being ready for Shabbas very early. "What do you gain from this *chumra* of yours," he asked, "other than to view others as *Shabbas* desecrators?"

"Those who *daven* a lengthy *Shemoneh Esrei* in a place where they prevent people from passing by," writes the *Steipler* Rav, "may think their fervent prayers are accumulating mitzvos. They are, in fact, guilty of wrongdoing since they are inconveniencing others!"

> During his last few days, Rabbi Shlomo Zalman Auerbach shared a room with a young *bochur* in Sha'arei Zedek Hospital. Late one night, Reb Shlomo Zalman suddenly jumped up in a panic and called for his nurse. He needed help in finding his alarm clock, explaining, "I'm afraid that the alarm will wake up my roommate."

The Mishna refers to the mitzva of helping another person as being "*nosei b'ol im chaveiro* (sharing your fellow's yoke)," whether physical, financial, spiritual, emotional or social. In other words, comfort in the form of whatever it takes to make a friend, relative or neighbor feel better.

This is derived from the concept of emulating God's ways, as we sing in *Tehillim* ("I am with him in distress"), quote from the Prophets ("In all their troubles He was troubled"), or find in Rabbi Yannai's conclusion ("Just as a twin feels pain when his twin suffers, so it is with the *Av Harachamim* and His people").

> When Rav Isser Zalman Meltzer was seriously wounded by the Jordanians during the 1948 War of Independence, he refused to scream for help because he didn't want to scare other Jews nearby, who were already in a state of panic. Instead, despite the pain and schrapnel in his leg, Rav Isser Zalman quietly hailed down an Israeli army jeep and had the soldiers drive him to the hospital.

Rabbi Chaim Shmulevitz, discussing the seriousness of causing anguish to others, claims that even if there was no intention of harm, the offender is still responsible!

> In his latter years, a few weeks before his passing, Rav Isser Zalman decided to begin *davening Shacharis k'vasikin* (at first light) so he asked Rav Ephraim Zileznik to wake him up at sunrise. Rav Ephraim woke his rebbe at the crack of dawn but Rav Isser decided to go back to his usual *minyan*. "I reconsidered," he explained. "For years now, there are Jews who are used to seeing me every morning at their *minyan* and they always wish me a good day. If I had stopped going they might feel uncomfortable. Therefore, I would rather forgo *davening k'vasikin* than cause another Jew, and certainly a whole group of Jews, even the slightest feeling of distress."

One of Benzion Abba Shaul's *chumros* was to avoid eating the cuts of meat that required the *nikkur* process, afraid that it might not be done properly. However, he would eat *nikkured* meat at his father-in-law's house, on the basis that not hurting another's feelings is more important than keeping a *chumra*.

As they were about to go to the matza bakery to make matza the *bochurim* of Rabbi Yisroel Salanter asked him what they should be concerned about. The father of the *mussar* movement reminded them that they should be careful not to hurt the feelings of the workers at the bakery, most of whom were widows.

The lesson is simple! You can't do a mitzva at the expense of another Jew.

It was a stifling hot day and a man fainted in the middle of a busy intersection in Boro Park. Traffic quickly piled up in all directions, so a woman rushed to help him. When she knelt down to loosen his collar, Moishie quickly pushed his way through the crowd, saying, "It's all right, honey, I've had a course in first aid."

The woman stood up and watched as Moishie took the ill man's pulse and prepared to administer artificial respiration. At this point she tapped him on the shoulder and said, "When you get to the part about calling a doctor, I'm already here!"

# Week 6

## On Being Content

"A slave is free if he is at peace with his lot;
a free man is a slave if he wants more!"

— *Yiddish folk saying*

Rabbi Mathias from Aish HaTorah relates, "I once asked a student of mine in Jerusalem, 'Would you rather be happy or rich?' He responded with a big smile, 'Why can't I have both?' 'Sure,' I told him, 'in a perfect world that's a nice answer, but let's get back to reality.' I pressed again, 'So what's it gonna be?'

"Without hesitation, he answered, 'Well, of course, Rabbi, I'd rather be happy than rich.'

"I said, 'OK, great, stay here in Jerusalem for a month and I'll teach you the secret of happiness.'

"He avoided eye contact as he replied, 'I don't know, Rabbi. A month is a long time and I have to get back to work.' Then I asked, 'Would you stay for a month if I gave you ten thousand dollars?'

"He answered right away, 'No problem!'

"I smiled and then asked, 'So tell me again, would you rather be happy or rich?'"

# Peace of Mind

> There was a king whose only daughter suffered from severe depression. The royal doctors informed the king that the only way she could be cured was by wearing the coat of a very happy person. So, the king sent messengers all over to find the happiest person in the kingdom. Finally they found someone in a tiny, distant village whom all the neighbors affirmed was the happiest man they had ever known.
>
> "Give us your coat," said the king's messengers, "and the king will reward you bountifully."
>
> "You don't understand," replied the happy man with a chuckle, "I don't have a coat! That is the secret of my happiness!"

The virtue of contentment is an elusive goal. Those who achieve it live in bliss; those who don't, in constant tension.

If you have too much, something is missing, say the Yiddishists. The more cynical amongst them were blunt: Everyone knows where his own shoe pinches!

It is true, they added: Everyone worries: some because they don't have enough pearls, others because they don't have enough beans in their soup!

Ben Sira, echoing the famous words of ben Zoma ("Who is rich? He who rejoices in his lot") summarizes it well: "With little or with much — be content!"

> When Rabbi Akiva married Rochel they were so poor they couldn't afford blankets so they slept under straw in a barn. One night, Eliyahu Hanavi, disguised as a beggar, came by and begged, "My wife is in labor. Can you spare some straw so I can cover her up?" Rabbi Akiva gave up his straw and turned to Rochel, and said, "See how fortunate we are to at least have straw to keep us warm!"

Commenting on Moshe's question to God, "Who am I, that I should go to Pharaoh?" and the reply, "When you bring the people out of Egypt and serve God on this mountain," the Ishbitzer Rebbe, Mordechai Yosef of Ishbitz, explains that one's identity is reflected in one's actions. You are not what you claim to be but what you do and how you feel about yourself!

"Who am I?" is not merely a question of name, age, address or occupation, but how one relates to others.

Contentment is visible in others. See if they are patient in their nature, demeanor and speech. The ability to remain calm at all times is the indispensable virtue for peace of mind. Here's a clue to tell if a *rav* has patience. Listen to the tone of his voice; soft-spokenness implies a calm interior, a man in control, one content with himself (note that the Rambam allows a "feigned anger" with one's children or students for disciplinary reasons, but only as long as the anger doesn't "penetrate the heart").

> Several years after Rabbi Salman Mutzapi moved to Eretz Yisroel from Iraq, several of his previous congregants came to visit him. Accustomed to affluence, they were shocked to see that their *rav* lived in a one-room apartment together with his whole family. Before they parted, they gave the family a gift of two thousand dinars. But Rav Salman refused, explaining, "How long do you think this money will last, two years? It cannot last forever. Therefore, I propose that instead of taking the money and having it run out in two years time, I will consider it as though you gave me the money two years ago and now it is depleted. Thank you very much!"

When Yaakov tells his brother, "*Ki chanani Elokim, v'chi yesh li kol* (God has been gracious to me, I have everything)," the *Kli Yakar* compares this to Esav's earlier response, wherein he says, "I have plenty."

Yaakov's response is one of contentment, in contrast to his brother's choice of words which implies that although he's wealthy, he needs more (the *If-I-have-one-hundred-I-need-two-hundred* syndrome).

The Torah understands human nature.

All the rivers run into the sea, observes *Koheles*, yet the sea is never full! Another verse: the eye is not satisfied with seeing, nor the ear with hearing!

As King Solomon put it: "Better a dry piece of bread with peace in it than a house full of contentious celebrations!"

Peace of mind that comes with being satisfied with one's lot is the mother of all blessings!

Being self-contented is also a critical prerequisite to showing concern for others. If you're happy, you want everybody to be happy.

When told of a man who had acquired great wealth, a wise man replied, "Has he also acquired the days in which to spend it?"

The cop pulls a car over and tells the driver he was going sixty miles per hour in a thirty-five mile-per-hour zone.

"I was only going thirty-five!" the driver starts yelling.

"Not according to my radar."

"Yes, I was!"

"No, you weren't!"

"Yes, I was!" the man screams, as his wife leans over to the annoyed cop and says, "Officer, I should warn you not to argue with my husband when he's been drinking!"

# Week 7

## On *Bikur Cholim*

There is no wealth like health!
— *Yiddish saying*

Rebbetzin Alte Faiga Teitelbaum, the Satmar Rav's wife, who had survived Bergen-Belsen, single-handedly brought the concept of an organized *bikur cholim* society to America. She began in her own kitchen, preparing fresh, nutritious meals, packaging them carefully and then catching trains to hospitals in Manhattan. Thin and frail but with a fierce determination, the rebbetzin would make her way from floor to floor, room to room, visiting Jewish patients. She would feed them, shmooze with them, wish them well, and go on to the next patient. Her borscht was legendary!

Reb Leibel Biztritsky, a prominent Lubavitcher Chassid, remembers sitting alone in a hospital, downcast and frightened. "Suddenly, the door opened, and there stood Reb Yoel's Rebbetzin, smiling as she offered me a freshly cooked meal. The Rebbetzin blessed me with a speedy recovery, and conversed with me for a few minutes. It was as if a ray of sunshine lit up my room. I felt renewed, refreshed, infused with fresh hope. The worthy Rebbetzin took the time to personally visit me. I have never forgotten that."

# The Infinite Mitzva

> It was *erev* Yom Kippur and Rav Moshe Feinstein suggested to Rabbi Lomner that they visit the Boyaner Rav. "He is very sick and on a day like today, he probably doesn't have any visitors since everyone is busy preparing for Yom Kippur." Indeed, they found the *rav* lying in bed all alone. Rav Moshe sat beside him and conversed with him as though he had all the time in the world. Rav Moshe finally stood up and wished the *rav*, who, by then, had a big smile on his face, a *refua shleima* and a good year.

The mitzva of *bikur cholim*, "visiting the sick," is modeled on the classic Midrash which portrays God visiting Avraham after his circumcision: "*V'halachta b'derachav* (you should walk in His ways, i.e., as He visited the sick, so shall you visit the sick)."

Remember: the parameters of *chesed* cannot be found in textbooks but are learned only by imitating role models of proper behavior. And, to eliminate any ambiguity, the Torah purposefully does not give any specific definition of a *choleh* (sick person), in order that the patient's condition not be a determining factor in whether to drop by and visit or not.

The reward for *bikur cholim*, according to Rav Yosef, is limitless, infinite. This mitzva is so unrestricted that, reminds Rava, you could do it a hundred times a day!

Rabbi Acha bar Chanina was convinced that *each* visit removes a sixtieth of a sick man's illness. And, interestingly, it is more incumbent on a prominent *rav* or recognized *talmid chacham* to do this mitzva than an ordinary layman. Why? Pain can be mitigated through *simcha*, therefore when visiting it's important to put a smile on a patient's face. If a *rosh yeshiva* comes to visit, a patient appreciates the special effort made for him and feels better for it.

> Whenever Rav Nosson Tzvi Finkel, the Alter of Slabodka, heard that someone he knew was ill, his daily routine changed completely. He prayed for the patient's recovery, arranged funds for private care, and researched who was the best doctor for that particular condition. If the sick person was one of his students, the entire Finkel family and every student in the yeshiva got involved in helping out. If a student showed any indifference, the *rosh yeshiva* didn't hesitate to rebuke him harshly.

*Bikur cholim* is not as simple as it sounds; it requires delicacy, skill, compassion and *seichel* (common sense, as not evidenced by the president of the *shul* who visits his *rav* in the hospital and says, "Rabbi, good news. Last night the board voted eight to two to wish you a *refua shleima!*").

Rabbi Yehuda Tzadka was never concerned about the time that it took to visit a sick person and always managed to do so. His very presence made the people he visited feel uplifted and hopeful, and he would part from the sick by showering them with blessings upon blessings.

When Rabbi Akiva found out his student was ill he not only went to visit him, but stretched the loving attention by cleaning the dirty floor in his room.

When the *Chazon Ish* heard one of his students had a throat disease, he didn't just visit but went and bought a bottle of honey for the boy.

Rabbi Akiva Eiger used to bring along some cake or cookies whenever he visited the sick. And he never left without asking for the patient's name and his mother's name, promising to pray on his behalf. If someone was needed to remain with a patient overnight, Rabbi Akiva Eiger would always personally volunteer.

Just showing up beside a hospital bed isn't all it takes.

You need to schedule your visits carefully, ask the patient what you can do to help, say a little prayer for him (specifically, a *Mishebeirach*, a plea to God for healing), be talkative (but let the patient take the lead), and be a good listener.

Here's what not to do: *don't* talk about the illness or anyone else's illness, *don't* expect to be entertained, *don't* talk about yourself but what the patient wants to talk about, *don't* sit on the bed, *don't* be afraid of silence, and *don't* be afraid to tell a joke: despite it being a *cliché*, laughter is, in fact, still one of the best medicines!

Whilst visiting his friend in the hospital, a man asked the patient what was wrong with him. After the illness was explained, he raised his hands aloft and sighed, "Oh, no! That's the same disease that killed my father!"

On hearing this, the patient became visibly disheartened and the visitor said, "Don't worry, I'm going to pray to God to make you better."

"While you're at it," the patient replied, "ask God if I may be saved from any more visits from idiots like you!"

# Week 8

## On Borrowing Money

Borrow, and you'll sorrow!
— *Yiddish folk saying*

Rav Yaakov Luberbaum's father-in-law, the *Nesivos Mishpat*, gave him a dowry that, if invested properly, could have lasted him a lifetime. Rav Yaakov wanted to spend his time learning Torah so he gave it to another to invest for him and send him a monthly dividend. Unfortunately, the businessman lost all the money in bad deals but, because of his respect for Rav Yaakov, promised to pay him back all the money.

"How can I take all the money at the expense of your other creditors?" Rav Yaakov replied. "There are specific guidelines of priority in terms of how money should be divided between a person's various creditors." Rav Yaakov then took whatever money he got back to the *beis din* and asked them to decide which creditors were entitled to the monies.

# Borrow to Banquet!

> Rabbi Chaim Soloveitchik once made a loan to a Jew but received nothing on the date of repayment. A few months later Rav Chaim met the debtor but, instead of apologizing for not paying, the man ridiculed Rav Chaim for having "completely forgotten" about the loan. Rav Chaim replied, "There is a shortcut from my home to *shul* which I have used for many years but, recently, I have chosen to go a longer way. Do you know why? Because using the shortcut means passing by your house. I have stopped going that way since the day I lent you money lest I accidentally transgress the Torah's injunction, 'Do not act toward him as a creditor.' So you see, I have never 'completely forgotten.' Only because I remember well that you owe me money and am afraid of transgressing a mitzva of the Torah do I spend more time than necessary making my way to *shul*!"

Once a loan has been made, one cannot act as a creditor to the borrower (*lo sihyeh lo k'nosheh*). Why not? The Midrash answers: "Do not treat him as a debtor," in order not to disturb another's self-esteem.

The *Ohr Hachaim* offers another reason: the money's not yours to begin with!

The Jew with "extra" money is no more than its caretaker until he gives it to its rightful owner, the poor and needy; therefore there can never be a "lending" borrower-creditor relationship.

That is why, when giving *tzedaka*, the giver must do so with a smile, since it is the recipient, explains the *Chasam Sofer*, who is granting *the giver* "the opportunity to fulfill this great mitzva."

When ben Sira saw Jews going into debt to pay for their *simchas*, he begged them not to "become a beggar from banqueting on borrowing!" When he saw Jews go into deep debt to build homes, he predicted their "gathering stones" would make good economic headstones.

The chassidic rebbe put it this way: If you carry your own lantern (i.e., don't borrow) you will survive the dark! The way to forestall misfortune, advise the rabbis of the Talmud, is not to depend on fortune!

> Rabbi Aryeh Levin was once summoned to court to pay a loan. Rav Aryeh was surprised because he couldn't remember signing his name as a guarantor. When he arrived he quickly discovered that his signature had been forged by a prominent member of the community. The debtor was in the room but was staring down at the floor, too ashamed to look Rav Aryeh in the eye. So Rav Aryeh decided not to challenge the debtor and paid off the

loan over the next few years, a loan he had never guaranteed — all in order to avoid humiliating the debtor!

Rav Huna, echoing *Mishlei*'s "The borrower is a slave to the lender," was so against debts that he said he would rather be hired out as a servant "in freedom" before becoming "enslaved" as a borrower.

Rav Meir Horowitz of Dzikov, grandson of Rav Naftoli of Ropshitz, would pray for his chassidim that when they come to him, their request should not be that he *daven* for their *parnassa*. Remember Jeremiah's bitter complaint? "I have not lent, neither have men lent to me; yet every one of them curses me!"

On borrowing, the *Mishlei Chachamin* has this to say: It brings concern by night and contempt by day! In dreams, goes a Yiddish saying, even fools get rich! But after acknowledging that you can't make cheesecake from snow, they add their opinion on wealth, bluntly: Quickly got, quickly lost!

> One day in *shul* the Gerer Rebbe, the Lev Simcha, realized he didn't have his wallet on him as the *gabbai* walked by with his *pushke* box. So the Rebbe turned to his assistant and asked him to "lend" him some money, even though the gabbai was carrying the Rebbe's money. When they returned home, the Gerer Rebbe took some money out of his wallet and returned the money to the *gabbai*.
>
> "I don't understand. The money is yours. Why are you returning your own money?"
>
> "A person must train himself that when he borrows he must repay!"

*Sefer Chassidim* warns: pay your debts — *before* you give charity!

Ibn Tibbon gets in the last word: "It's better to retire without supper, and rise without debt!"

When I was a young boy I used to think that if you were very nice to very rich people they would give you fabulous presents, like a Cadillac or a house on the French Riviera. But as I journeyed through life I discovered that rich people give you nothing — that's why they're rich!

— *Groucho Marx*

# Week 9

## On Bribery, Justice

*Better to suffer an injustice than commit one.*
— *Yiddish folk saying*

The famous Shach was once involved in a *din Torah* between two communities. Each community sent a *rav* from their own town and a third rabbi was chosen to hear the case and rule accordingly. The Shach represented his town, and, to the shock of everybody, the third rabbi ruled against him. "I am surprised by your decision," the Shach said to the rabbi, "since the Gemora implies otherwise…"

"Yes, I am familiar with that Gemora, and, at first, I was under the impression that it was quite relevant to the case at hand. However, I recently came across a new *sefer* named *Sifsei Cohen* (authored by the Shach, the *sefer* for which he is known), which discredits its relevance to this matter!"

Upon hearing this, the Shach was stunned. He could not believe that he would have forgotten something that he himself had written. It was then that he realized how a bias can totally distort one's thinking!

# Law and Disorder

> It was a terrible thunderstorm and Rav Shlomo Shimshon Karelitz, *dayan* of Petach Tikva, was walking down the street struggling to hold onto his hat and briefcase. A *to'ein* (a rabbinical advocate), driving by, recognized the *rav*. "I urged him to quickly get into the car," recalled the *to'ein*, "but as soon as he identified me, he refused, explaining, 'I appreciate the offer, but you are a *to'ein*, I cannot accept a favor from you. Who knows what you might tell me along the way that could affect my judgment?'" And Rav Shlomo Shimshon continued walking home in the torrential rain!

"If you grease the wheels, you can ride!" says a character from a Sholem Aleichem play.

Not so in a Judaism that considers bribery as sheer evil. And if evil is allowed to enter as a guest, notes a Midrash, it soon becomes the host!

When judging a case, Jewish judges must remember that they are *also* on trial. Those who judge truthfully, says the Talmud, "even for a single hour," have become joint-venture partners with God in the ongoing creation of a better world.

Therefore judges cannot accept gifts or bribes (*V'shochad lo sikach*) even, explains Rashi, if they still intend to rule truthfully, because distortion in truth and unfair favoritism become inevitable ("A judge who accepts a bribe and alters the verdict will go blind!").

> As the *maggid* was presiding over a *din Torah* that involved a relative of the Ba'al Shem Tov, the Besht accidentally walked into the room. The *maggid* was so concerned that his revered Rebbe's presence might influence him that, without hesitating for a moment, he declared, "In the name of the court I request that whoever does not need to be in the room at this time should please leave!"

One day, a famous elderly *dayan* was boarding a fishing boat and a passenger instinctively stuck out his hand to help him. At a later date, the Jew appeared before the *dayan* in a *din Torah* and the *dayan* recused himself — because of this small favor!

Rav Shlomo Kluger once received *mishloach manos* on Purim from a certain individual, as the *minhag* was to send *mishloach manos* to the *rav*. Rav Kluger sensed that that year's offering was a bit nicer than those of earlier years. Several months later, that person approached Rav Kluger with a *din Torah*. Rav Kluger refused to participate on the grounds that the fancier *mishloach manos* constituted *shochad*.

Rav Elchonon Wassermann discusses whether the size of the bribe makes a difference. No, he concludes, defining the minimum amount as a *shoveh pruta*, "less than a penny;" the same amount that defines stealing or taking interest.

Rav Shlomo Wolbe reminds us that it only takes one (small) gram to tip a scale and only the slightest degree of bias to affect a court case. Think twice, urges the Vilna Gaon: "What gives you pleasure today will give you tears tomorrow!"

> During the time that he served as *av beis din* of Turtchin, Poland, the Rebbe, Rav Yechiel Alexander, presided over a *din Torah* at which his disciple, Rav Aron Flint, served as mediator. On the day of the *din Torah*, Rav Aron arrived in Turtchin and went to see his mentor. He extended his arm to greet Rav Yechiel, but the latter did not return the courtesy until after the conclusion of the case.

The Torah is so sensitive to even unintentional favoritism that it even requires both litigants to dress comparably; if a rich man shows up in ostentatious robes he has to pay to clothe the other litigant to look similar, or himself change into simple clothes like his opponent.

> The Maharil Diskin was so afraid of favoring one litigant over the other that he refused to act as a judge unless both parties agreed to present their case to him while standing behind a closed door. He was afraid that by looking at them he would already pass a subconscious judgement, which could hinder his issuance of the absolute truth.

"One must accept the truth from whatever source," says the Rambam. Adds Moshe ibn Ezra: even a liar tells the truth now and then!

At the height of a major criminal trial, the prosecuting attorney attacks Moishie, a witness for the defendant.

"Isn't it true," he bellows, "that you accepted five thousand dollars to compromise this case?"

Moishie just stares out the window, as though he hasn't heard the question.

"Isn't it true that you accepted five thousand dollars to compromise this case?" the lawyer shouts again. Moishie still doesn't respond.

Finally, the judge leans over and says, "Sir, please answer the question."

"Oh," Moishie says, "I thought he was talking to you!"

# Week 10

## On *Chesed shel Emes*, Eulogies

"Show up for the inheritance and you
may have to pay for the funeral!"

— *Yiddish folk saying*

While Rabbi Yisroel Slanter was living in Kovno, a poor, elderly woman passed away. In Kovno, there were two *chevra kaddishas*, one officially belonging to Kovno and the other to the adjacent Slabodka. Unfortunately, the two organizations disputed whose responsibility it was to undertake this woman's burial. Each group claimed it was the duty of the other.

It so happened that their argument took place in the *beis medrash* while Rav Yisroel Salanter was *davening Shacharis* and was about to begin the *Shemoneh Esrei*. Upon hearing the subject under debate, Rav Yisroel stopped *davening* immediately, removed his *tallis* and *tefillin* and called to several of his students to join him in the mitzva of burying the dead.

"It is a halacha," proclaimed Rav Yisroel, "that a person who dies leaving no one to look after his funeral is considered a *mes mitzva* (an obligatory corpse). In that case, all other mitzvos are pushed aside for this one!"

# The Most *Bona Fide* Mitzva of Them All

On one of his visits to Yerushalayim, Rav Yoel Teitelbaum wasn't feeling well and the doctors recommended that he remain indoors. But after a few days the Satmar Rav, although not feeling any better, decided to pay a *shiva* call to Rabbi Tzvi Eichler. Since he was leaving the house anyway he was asked if he would also visit a patient at Sha'arei Zedek Hospital. The Satmar Rav declined, saying it was too strenuous for him, and that being *menachem aveil* was more important because it "benefited both the mourner and the soul of the *niftar*." However, when he finished his *shiva* call the *rav* had a change of heart and dropped in at the hospital to do *bikur cholim*, despite his own weakened state.

So what takes precedence? Comforting mourners (*nichum aveilim*) or visiting the sick?

The Rambam favors the former, because "it is an act of kindness to both the living and the dead." But the *Ridvaz* throws in a caveat: "If one neglects visiting the sick it is as though he takes his life away; visiting him revives him!"

"Deal kindly and truly (with *chesed v'emes*) with me," Yaakov asks of his son, Yosef, referring to his burial.

Rashi explains that adding the word *true* after *kindness* is an acknowledgment that since the dead can offer no reciprocal gesture, this is kindness in its "truest" sense, defined by the *Chofetz Chaim* as a *bona fide* mitzva of kindness (*chesed shel emes*).

It's a mistake to assume that *chesed v'emes* only relates to *kavod hameis*.

The *Sifsei Chachamim* extends it to cover any good deed where there is no expectation of a reward. "Don't be like servants who serve on the condition of receiving a reward," writes the Mishna's Antigonos ish Socho. "Rather, be like servants who serve unconditionally!"

The *hesped* (eulogy) is derived from the verse *"Arah v'livkosa* ([Avraham] came to eulogize [Sarah] and to bewail her)." It is, according to Rabbi Elazar Azcari, a part of the mitzva of *gemilus chasadim*, "bestowing kindness."

Tears are a sign of grief, counted and gathered by God ("Place my tears in Your flask"). But excessive mourning is inappropriate, a suggestion that God's judgment is flawed; and be warned: false, phony praises at eulogies are frowned upon, no matter how good the orator!

> Prior to his death, the humble Rav Yehuda Hanasi (Rebbe) surprised everyone by asking that he not be eulogized only in small villages but also in larger towns. Rabbi Chaim Dovid Halevi explains the unusual request: "The main reason for eulogizing the dead is for the deceased himself. When a person dies, God says to the angels, '[Go] see what the people say about him.' He who is pleasing to man is pleasing also to God. Rebbe's request was thus an extension of his supreme modesty. He genuinely feared the Heavenly judgment, and consequently sought a wellspring of support in this world, through the many *hespedim* that would be delivered on his behalf."

Many great sages preferred not to be eulogized, including Rav Aaron of Karlin and Rav Shmuel Salant; nevertheless, Rabbi Chaim Berlin got up and enumerated Rav Salant's qualities in order to perform *bechi* ("shedding tears") at the great loss that *Klal Yisroel* had suffered, which he said was an acceptable thing to do at a funeral.

Rabbi Chaim David Halevy points out that giving a hesped is only one of three good deeds that the *Shulchan Aruch* calls a *mitzva gedola*, "a great mitzva" (the other two are *pidyon shevuyim*, "redemption of captives," and *halva'a la'aniyim*, "lending money to the poor").

> The tzadik of Peshischa lay on his death bed, his wife by his side, crying bitterly. "Why are you weeping?" asks the Rebbe, "I have been given an entire life simply so I might be taught to die!" In other words: "Make plans in this world as if you hope to live forever," urges Solomon ibn Gabirol, "but make plans for the World to Come as if you expect to die tomorrow!"

Rav Nissan Alpert describes the purpose of *hesped*: "To 'bring the dead to life,' by recounting his praises and good deeds, so that people will learn from him."

This link of *hesped* to *teshuva* is why the Rav, J. B. Soloveitchik, titled one of his lectures "Sitting Shiva Is Doing Teshuva"!

At the local cemetery is a tombstone that reads:

> Remember man, as you walk by,
> As you are now, so once was I.
> As I am now, so shall you be.
> Remember this and follow me.

Under which, someone scribbled:

> To follow you I'll not consent…
> Until I know which way you went!

# Week 11

## On Clarity in Teaching Torah

*Think and thank!*
— *Yiddish folk saying*

A *talmid chacham* in B'nei Brak once asked a Torah scholar, presumably Rav Chaim Kanievsky, how many times Moshe appears in the Torah. The scholar answered, "614 times" (the significance of "614" is 613 for all the mitzvos, plus one: Moshe, who was *k'neged kol haTorah*, equal to the whole Torah!). No, the man replied, it appears 616 times. The scholar smiled and replied that he must have gotten that number from a computer, which doesn't have the same clarity as a human. The computer included, he explained, two words (*miseh*, "from the sheep," and *mashe*, "to lend") that have the same letters as Moshe but are pronounced differently.

# What? Say That Again?

> Before beginning his *shiur* in Gemora, the *Chasam Sofer* used to review the appropriate *mishna* over and over again. With his finger on the words, he would read the line slowly and clearly, each time as though he had never seen the words before, whether he was learning with students or alone. For the same reason, after delivering his *shiur*, the *Chasam Sofer* reviewed it to himself at least four more times.

After Moshe complains that he is not a speaker, his brother Aaron, with the ability to clarify, becomes God's spokesman. From that moment on, clarity in education was key.

In his *Sefer Sha'ashuim*, the Barcelena scholar Yosef Zabara defined clarity as being able to "be brief without repeating." But remember: a little light is precious, too much is blinding!

Clarity to teach Torah requires patience ("An edgy person cannot teach!"). Haste leads to confusion, misunderstanding and frustration.

Don't hire a short-tempered rebbe, warns Rav Yehuda Hachassid; not even if he is truly dedicated, adds Rav Aaron Kotler, because his personality defect will stunt the growth of his students.

There are already many impediments to a child's development, notes Rav Eliezer Papo, so we need not add one more, that of an impatient rebbe!

"A rebbe must be compassionate, patient, full of kindness," elaborates Rav Shlomo Wolbe, "and tolerate a degree of misconduct."

> Rabbi Yehoshua Leib Diskin once gave a very complex *shiur* to his most advanced students. There was a layman at the *shiur* who later approached Rav Yehoshua Leib, saying that he had not understood most of it. Rav Yehoshua Leib sat down with him and slowly and clearly explained each step along the way until the man understood the *shiur*. The students were in awe at how much effort their rebbe was putting into patiently explaining the material to a layman.

Rav Shlomo Zalman Auerbach, in his characteristically simple style, would explain and re-explain the material being studied if a student had difficulty grasping it. "Open your mouth, and let your words be clear," states the Talmud in all its blunt clarity.

Rav Elchonon Wasserman always delivered his *shiur* in a clear, concise fashion, his students sensing how *each word* was calculated to lend meaning to the whole.

"A good teacher," Rav Elchonon clarified, "is one whose explanation lacks no word necessary to clarify the subject."

"The main thing is for a rebbe to be perceptive enough to understand not only the material he is teaching, but also to understand his students," wrote Rav Tzvi Pesach Frank, rabbi of Yerushalayim. "In order to teach others, one must understand his students' way of thinking and pinpoint what exactly they are having difficulty grasping."

The only effective way to teach Torah, argued Rav Yeruchem Levovitz, the *Mirer mashgiach*, is for the rebbe to first eliminate all ulterior motives and focus purely on the needs of the students. The finest quality of a rebbe, according to Rav Ezra Attiya, *rosh yeshiva* of *Porat Yosef*, is an ability to tailor his words not to his own wisdom but to the intelligence level of his students.

> The Talmud relates: "Rabbi Abbahu and Rabbi Chiya came to the same town at the same time. Rabbi Chiya delivered a scholarly discourse on the Law, while Rabbi Abbahu delivered a midrashic sermon. Afterward all the people left Rabbi Chiya and came to Rabbi Abbahu. Rabbi Chiya was seriously discouraged, but his colleague said to him, "I will tell you a parable. Two men entered the same village, the one offering to sell precious gems and pearls, the other costume jewelry. To whom do you think the people rushed? Of course it was the man selling costume jewelry, for that was what the people could afford to purchase!"

The genius in teaching Torah is the ability to "lower oneself" to the needs of the audience. This is not easy to do. Those who master this technique are stepping not "lower" but *beyond* their genius because their technique allows them to teach Torah to each individual student.

One of the most essential things for a Torah scholar, notes Rav Shlomo Luria, "is to write even an ordinary letter in clear language!"

The Rambam gets the final say: "Concerning words of Torah, the speaker's words should be few but his content rich. He should teach students calmly, patiently, without raising his voice, without being too wordy."

Now that's clarity!

Saul was taking an oral exam during his test for citizenship and was asked to use the word "cultivate" in a sentence.

With a big smile, he answered: "Last vinter on a very cold day, I vas vaiting for a bus, but it vas too cultivate, so I took the subvay home!"

# Week 12

## On Commerce — Wages and Prices

> The harder I work, the luckier I get!
> — *Yiddish folk saying*

One day Reb Yisroel Salanter and his friend stopped at a small *shul* on a side street in Vilna to daven *Mincha*. While his friend washed his hands as usual, Reb Yisroel used only a few drops of water.

"Are you not particular to wash your hands before davening?" asked the friend.

"I usually am. However, I'm afraid that this small *shul* has a regular number of *mispallelim* and that they seldom have guests. If the *shammes* brought in only enough water for the regulars and we use too much water, the shortage might cause the *gabbai* to blame the *shammes* for failing to bring enough water and might consequently reduce his wages. In that case, my stringency could conceivably cost someone his livelihood."

# A Hard Day's Night

> One *erev Shabbas*, the *Chofetz Chaim* was seen running down the street just a few minutes before candle lighting. Apparently one of the men who printed his *seforim* had rushed home for Shabbas before the *Chofetz Chaim* could pay him. Not wanting to delay payment until *motzei Shabbas*, the *Chofetz Chaim* ran to the worker's house to fulfill the mitzva of *b'yomo siten s'choro*, "On that day you shall pay his hire," before lighting *Shabbas* candles.

When Rav Shaul Broch of Kashoi gave his *sifrei Torah* to a *sofer* for inspection he was quoted a price for the entire job. A few hours later, Rav Shaul returned and told the *sofer*, "I've changed my mind. I do not want to pay you by the job but by the hour so that every day I can fulfill the mitzva, 'On that day you shall pay his hire.'"

And so it was; every day before *Mincha* for the next two years or so, Rav Shaul paid the *sofer* for that day's work in fixing his *sifrei Torah*.

> Rav Salman Mutzapi was working long hours and his friend asked him why. "Well," explained Rav Salman, "next week is my wedding, and I won't be working for an entire week. Therefore, I am making up the hours ahead of time by working late into the night."
> 
> "But surely you are entitled to a few days of paid vacation?"
> 
> "Yes, but I prefer not to benefit from that which I have not earned!"

Both employers and employees have responsibilities to each other, and both are rewarded for good behavior. Remember: Yaakov became "exceedingly prosperous" *because* he worked diligently for Lavan.

Sensitivity in the work force regulates all types of conduct (you cannot use false weights and measures, you must allow a worker in the field to eat from the produce he is harvesting, etc.), and the Ramchal reminds the worker that his hours belong to his boss, not to him.

The employee cannot even interrupt his work to do a mitzva — and if he does, it's "theft" (stealing hours from his employer) and therefore a nullified mitzva. Can he strike? Yes. The Talmud encourages craftsmen to organize themselves union-wise, and even allows them to democratically decide for themselves their own fair wages and prices.

In one ruling, the Rambam ruled that wages must be increased even if "he [the employee] objects to the increase!"

> A shoemaker once returned a pair of shoes to Rabbi Chaim Chezkia M'dini,

author of *Sdei Chemed*, but the *rav* only had a large bill on him and the shoemaker had no change.

"That's okay," said the shoemaker, "I will come back tomorrow to get the money."

"Absolutely not!" cried Rabbi Chaim Chezkia. "The Torah says that one may not delay a worker's payment overnight, and I will not let you suffer because I can't get change." Instead, Rabbi Chaim Chezkia borrowed the cost of the repair from a third person so that he could fulfill the mitzva of paying a worker's wages on time.

The *Kav Hayashar* defines nonpayment of a worker as a *chilul Hashem*, "a manifestation of pure callousness."

Is it a coincidence?

The famous Talmudic phrase *lifnim mishurat hadin*, which encourages Jews to go "beyond the strict letter of the law," is the concluding part of the Torah's stipulation that the boss must pay his employees in a fair and equitable way.

After the Gerer Rebbe, Rav Simcha Bunim Alter, discovered that the construction of Yeshivas Chiddushei HaRim in Tel Aviv was over budget and the builder was not being paid, the Rebbe called the builder at five a.m. at home and asked that they meet at the local bank in a few hours. The Rebbe then made a special trip from Yerushalayim and told him, "I could not sleep all night. It reminded me of the *pasuk* '*Lo solin pe'ulas sochir itcha ad boker* (A worker's wages will not let you sleep until the morning)!'" The Rebbe then withdrew a large sum of money from his own account to pay the man what he was owed.

Whoever withholds an employee's wages, say the rabbis of the Talmud, "it is as though he has taken the person's life from him."

Or in Yiddish: You never work so hard as when you're not being paid for it!

A business owner decides to take a tour around his business and see how things are going. He goes down to the shipping docks and sees a young man leaning against the wall doing nothing. The owner walks up to the young man and says, "Son, how much do you make a day?"

The guy replies, "A hundred fifty dollars."

The owner pulls out his wallet, gives him $150, and tells him to get out and never come back.

A few minutes later, the shipping clerk asks the owner, "Have you seen the UPS driver? I asked him to wait here for me!"

# Week 13

## On Conflict, Controversy

Two farmers each claim to own a particular cow.
While one of the farmers pulls at the cow's head, and the
other yanks at the tail, the cow gets milked by a lawyer.

— *Yiddish folk saying*

Rav Meir Horowitz of Dzikov, grandson of Rav Naftoli of Ropshitz, refused to get involved in conflict. One year there was a disagreement between Sanz and Sadigora over the ostentatious lifestyle of the Sadigora Rebbe. The Rebbe argued in his defense that his way of living increased people's respect for Torah and its teachers. The Sanzer Rebbe disagreed, convinced that *gedolim* should live humbly.

When asked for his opinion Rav Meir responded with a parable about the lion that strolled through the forest asking the animals whether he had bad breath. Any animal that replied "yes" was instantly killed for insulting the king of the forest, and any animal that answered "no" was killed for lying. However, when the fox was asked for its opinion, it evaded trouble by replying, "I have a cold and cannot smell!" — and lived.

The same applies to us, explained Rav Meir to his chassidim, "concerning this Sanz-Sadigora dispute, we are all suffering from colds and cannot smell and decide who is right. This way, we will keep out of trouble!"

# Time Out!

> The Gerer Rebbe, Rav Avraham Mordechai, was distressed over a rift between two rabbis, one of whom bore an age-old grudge against the other for humiliating him many years earlier. Nothing the *Imrei Emes* said to the rabbi could convince him to change his mind. Suddenly, the Rebbe drew a letter from inside his jacket and passed it to the rabbi to read. He began to read a line or two when his face became contorted, and he stopped reading.
>
> "Carry on," insisted the Gerer Rebbe, "I want you to read until the end."
>
> The letter had been written by someone who was very upset with the Gerer Rebbe, and it was filled with curses and insults against the Rebbe.
>
> "I received this letter many years ago, even before my father passed away," explained the Rebbe. "The writer is a businessman, and he was under the impression that I had done him an injustice. From the day I received this letter, I have read it each morning before *davening*, and, each time, I tell *Hashem* that I forgive the man wholeheartedly. Then I pray that he be well and that he not be punished for his error."

The Talmud has a litmus test on how to tell which Jew came from good lineage: watch an argument and the one who stays silent has the finer background.

Even if it takes a lifetime, urges the Talmud, one should try to replace the coarseness of confrontation with the humility of gentleness.

When the Torah recalls episodes of confrontation, points out the *Kli Yakar*, it often ignores the names of those in dispute because the very fact they're arguing means they have an inherently flawed family tree. Rav takes this as marriage advice: when seeking a partner choose one from a "quieter family" with a quiet nature ("Abstention from quarrel is a man's honor!").

> When he dropped in to visit Rav Yechezkel Abramsky, the Jew was shocked to see the *rav* lying in his bed, crying bitterly. "What happened?" he asked. Rav Yechezkel explained that earlier that day he had been sitting on the bus going home to Bayit Vegan when he saw two Jews in the street arguing, punching each other. This had upset him so much that, hours later, he was still crying over what he had witnessed!

The Tzartkover Rebbe gave no sermons nor talks. His confused chassidim finally begged him for an explanation. "There are seventy ways to teach Torah," the Rebbe replied, "and one of the paths is through silence!"

Rav Yitzchak Abuhav, author of *Menoras Hamaor*, always ran from confrontation, quoting Solomon's wisdom: "A righteous man has an advantage over his fellow [because] the way of the wicked leads them astray!"

> Whenever Rav Yisroel Salanter was involved in a debate regarding the proper understanding of a Gemora, he always made an effort to allow his opponent, *talmid chacham* or not, to have the last word. Even if he had a way to answer the person's difficulties, he preferred to give the man the good feeling that he had "beaten" Rav Yisroel in a Torah discussion.

Not getting in the last word requires discipline, and a strong aversion to argumentation. Remember: a man's tongue is often his worst enemy!

Shimon ben Chalafta thought it was a blessing from God to "neither shame nor be shamed."

Shimon bar Yochai thought it was better to throw yourself into a blazing fire than to shame another in public, which the Talmud equates to "shedding blood"!

> The Sassover Rebbe told his disciples to endure the pain of insult silently, whilst the Vizhnitzer Rebbe, author of *Damesek Eliezer*, advised his chassidim not to waste their time challenging those who abuse them. Remaining silent in the face of insult (*shomeia cherposo v'eino meishiv*), writes Rav Zundel Salant to his son, is such a supreme mitzva that it can revoke evil decrees.

After *Sefer Chassidim* urged that it's better to tell a white lie than get into a fight by insulting another, Jewish law allowed certain "white lie" exceptions. These three are areas where it may be permissible to bend the truth: how much a person has learned (*meseches*), details of one's private life (*puria*), and information on one's hosts (*ushpiza*).

Even then, notes the *Ben Ish Chai*, *chachamim* are careful not to tell an outright lie but to give an ambiguous response. This cleverness, asserted Rav Ezra Attiya, differentiates a *talmid chacham* from an absolute *talmid chacham*!

Sidney arrives home at his usual 6.30 p.m. time, takes off his coat, sits down in his favorite chair, opens the newspaper, and calls out to his wife, "Leah, I'm home, can you make me a cup of tea before it starts?"

Leah makes him a cup of tea. As soon as he's finished his tea Sidney calls out to her again, "Can I have another cup of tea? I think it's going to start very soon."

This time his wife is annoyed, but still makes him another cup of tea. When he empties that cup, he again asks his wife for a third cup, "before it starts."

"That's the last straw," Leah yells back. "You're a rude, inconsiderate lowlife. You come home, don't say one word to me, make yourself comfortable, and then expect me to act like your servant. Doesn't it ever occur to you that I might be tired, with all the cleaning, washing, ironing, shopping and cooking I do to keep this house of ours spotlessly clean? I don't think you ever give me a thought. Selfish, that's what you are. You don't need a wife, you need a slave, you need someone to -"

"Oh, oh," Sidney sighs, "it's started!"

# Week 14

## On *Da'as Torah*

If you insist you're right long enough, you'll be wrong.
— *Yiddish folk saying*

A woman without children once went to Rabbi Moshe Feinstein, zt"l, and said to him, "For years now, my husband has been coming to you for a *bracha* that we be blessed with children. However, our prayers still have not been answered. Therefore, I request that the *Rosh Yeshiva* make a declaration that we will have children, for, as *chazal* say, "A *tzadik* declares and HaKadosh Boruch Hu fulfills."

"You want me to make such a statement?" asked Rav Moshe. "What power do my words have in this regard?"

"Yes, the *Rosh Yeshiva* can make such a statement…you can…" said the woman with tears rolling down her cheeks. Then she began to cry so bitterly that Rav Moshe finally said to her, "I can't make such statements, but one thing I can say is that seeing your utter faith in the rabbis, you definitely *deserve* a child."

Those words certainly brought comfort to the brokenhearted woman. With pure faith, she believed that her request was destined to be fulfilled. "When?" she asked Rav Moshe innocently.

Rav Moshe thought for a moment and replied, "Immediately after Chanuka."

Indeed, on the last day of the next Chanuka, the woman went into labor and gave birth to a baby boy that evening.

# When Right Is Left

> Once, the Netziv of Volozhin tripped in *shul* whilst carrying a *sefer Torah*. The crowd immediately rushed to pick up the *sefer Torah*. From the rear of the *shul* shouted out a cry. It was Rav Yitzchak of Volozhin, the Netziv's son-in-law. "Pick up the Netziv first and then the *sefer Torah*. Men who rise up before a *sefer Torah* but not a Torah sage are foolish. A *talmid chacham* is a living *sefer Torah* and thus takes precedence over a *sefer Torah* of parchment!"

Originally, the term *da'as Torah*, literally "Torah knowledge" (in contrast to *da'as nota*, "personal opinion"), was used in the Gemora, where it appears only once, in a different context than today. A person once asked a *Tanna* whether his opinion on a halachic matter was deduced from logic and traditional sources, or whether it was his own personal opinion as shaped by his *da'as Torah*.

A *talmid chacham* once asked the *Chazon Ish* the following question: If one were to take a spoonful of food out of a pot that is on the stove on Shabbas and then put the spoon back inside the pot to take out another spoonful, would that be a problem of *chazora* (putting food back on the fire on Shabbas)? The *Chazon Ish* replied it was permissible and then asked, with a smile, "Would you ask *da'as Torah* such nitty-gritty questions about the *halachos* of *loshen hora* as well?"

"Many people," explained Rabbi Shlomo Zalman Auerbach, mistakenly think that Torah scholars are like a watch. A watch tells time, a scholar tells Torah. A watch, though, is not inherently time. In the same way, a *talmid chacham* is not inherently "the Torah."

However, *chazal* teach us that a person who learns the holy Torah *lishma* (for its own sake) receives sanctity from within the Torah itself and becomes "a living *sefer Torah*."

It is assumed that Torah sages, with the advantage of being guided by Heaven, must naturally have a greater understanding of God's will and thus, infused with the advantage of *ruach hakodesh* (Divine inspiration), act as the best-qualified leaders for the Jewish people.

This of course is not the same as infallibility. That's the *other* religion! Or as the Yiddishists would put it: Just because a goat has a beard that doesn't make him a rabbi!

> The Steipler Rav's grandson once asked his grandfather, "What if I ask a *rav* a question on a subject he knows nothing about? Am I to consider his reply as *da'as Torah*?"

> "Most certainly!" came the reply. "Any question that is answered by a *talmid chacham* who is absorbed in his learning must be regarded as *da'as Torah*, and his word must be heeded!"

And yet: the Talmud advises rabbis to leave military questions…to the generals!

> After his doctor told him not to eat anything that lingered on uncooked because of his serious ulcer problem, a Jew asked the *Chofetz Chaim* whether he could eat *cholent* on Shabbas, since it was cooked the day before. The *Chofetz Chaim* told him that anything eaten in honor of Shabbas will not be harmful.
> "But Rebbe, I'm worried about my health."
> "Then it's best you follow the doctor's orders," replied the *Chofetz Chaim*, explaining that those who are uncomfortable in accepting the words of our Sages as plain truth have, by definition, reason to be concerned.

If we have difficulty understanding the words of the Sages, Rabbi Eliezer Papo blames that on "our small-mindedness that inhibits us from grasping the depths of their understanding!"

> The Tzupenester Rebbe discovered his followers playing a game of checkers and told them, "It is possible to achieve much learning by observing the rules of this game. You must give up one in order to take two; it is impossible to make two moves at one time; you are allowed to move up but not down; once you have reached the top, then you can move where you want!"

This a central tenet of Judaism: to follow the counsel of elders as a rudimentary element of faith in God, even if they tell you that right is left and left is right.

Rav Moshe Aron Stern, the *mashgiach* of Kaminetz, approached this strange expression from the logic of perspective. What is right for one person is left for the person standing opposite him; the same is true for one's perception of right and wrong. Only the wise elders of the nation, fusing Torah knowledge with their vast experience, have the correct perspective.

A *cheder* rebbe decided to give the math class. He points to Beryl and says, "Beryl! If you reached in your right pocket and found a dollar and then you reached in your left pocket and found another one, what would you have?"

"Somebody else's pants!"

# Week 15

## On *Derech Eretz*, Respect

*The best ability is respectability!*
— *Yiddish folk saying*

One day in the Slabodka Yeshiva a student saw a piece of paper on the floor and bent down to pick it up, thinking it was *sheimos* (materials with God's name printed in them, which require special disposal). When he realized it was simply a scrap of ordinary paper, he dropped it right back on the floor. Rav Nosson Tzvi Finkel, the Alter of Slabodka, saw him do this and was shocked at the lack of *derech eretz*. "How dare you leave this stumbling block on public property? You are causing detriment to all who pass by!" When Rav Nosson Tzvi saw that the boy was surprised at his reaction, he explained that a stumbling block is not only a brick or a pothole that can cause someone physical harm.

"By dropping the piece of paper on the floor," said the Alter, "you are causing the next person who passes by to bend down and pick it up. In doing so you not only cause him to exert himself unnecessarily, but you also waste the time of another student on his way to study Torah. Nothing can be more harmful and disrespectful than that. I know that you did not throw the paper here in the first place, but, nevertheless, once you picked it up and threw it back down you recreated the obstruction. The Gemora teaches that if one rolls a stone that was already on public property, he is responsible for any damage that results. This is because he uprooted the first person's action and re-created the obstruction!"

# What's Yours Is Mine!

> On his way to a wedding, Rav Shneur Kotler asked his driver to be ready to leave immediately after the *chuppa* because he had a very important meeting to attend that night. However, the *rav* did not emerge immediately from the wedding hall, and the driver waited and waited until Rav Shneur finally came out. "What happened?" the driver asked.
>
> "Well," Rav Shneur replied, "I was not given a *bracha* at the *chuppa*, nor any *kibbud*, therefore if I had run out the *ba'al simcha* and his family would have thought I left offended. This would have interfered in his *simcha* and caused a *shvere hartz* on the night of his child's *chasuna* — so I couldn't leave!"

Lack of respect for others is a form of arrogance, a direct result of self-centeredness.

Rav Aaron Kotler was convinced that those who think only about their own needs will eventually not even concede that which rightfully belongs to others (a what's-yours-is-mine attitude).

A Midrash claims that *derech eretz* "comes before Torah," in that no Jew can sustain a life of Torah in the absence of proper, respectful, thoughtful, polite, civilized behavior.

In fact, the entire body of *mussar* teachings rests on this principle, that *middos* ("[good] character traits") are a prerequisite to Torah.

> In 1949, the Gerer Rebbe went to visit the *Chazon Ish*. When the visit was over, the *Chazon Ish* rose to escort his guest to a waiting taxi. As they neared the end of the path, Reb Yisroel Alter turned around to accompany the *Chazon Ish* back to his door. However, as soon as they reached the door, the *Chazon Ish* duly turned around to walk him back to the taxi. This happened several times. In the end, the Gerer Rebbe walked his host all the way into the house. Then he quickly closed the door and ran to the car so that the *Chazon Ish* would not have a chance to follow him.

The term *derech eretz* literally means "the way of the land," and is inherently ambiguous.

"Beautiful is the study of Torah with *derech eretz*," writes *Pirkei Avos*, "as involvement with both makes one forget sin."

In this context, *derech eretz*, in short "respect," can mean either making a livelihood (according to the Rambam) or simply good manners (according to the philosophy of *mussar*).

Once, after a large public gathering, Rav Moshe Feinstein began making his way to an important meeting of *talmidei chachamim*. He stopped suddenly when he came across a man davening *Shemoneh Esrei*. To walk in front of him was, of course, forbidden, and there was no alternative route, so Rav Moshe just waited. After some time, Rav Moshe's *gabbai* began to pressure him, reminding him that the other rabbis were waiting.

"What can I do?" asked Rav Moshe. "There is a wall in front of me!"

In his famous *Commentary to Leviticus*, Rav Shimshon Raphael Hirsch, who was famously a proponent of *"Torah im Derech Eretz,"* makes it clear that Torah is the *ikkar* (essential), and all other knowledge is *tofel* (secondary). The Torah's idea of *derech eretz*, or respect, is that it applies to…everything, from (live) people to (dead) objects to (mute) animals, ever since God asked the evildoing prophet Bilam, who wanted to curse the Jewish people, "Why did you strike your donkey?"

One evening, Rebbetzin Lopian, the "yeshiva mother," became alarmed after seeing some mice scurrying around in the storage room. Rav Dovid Yosef Shlosberg instructed several boys to set up a cat in the corner to "guard" the food. A few days later, the *rosh yeshiva*, Rav Eliyahu Lopian, noticed the cat and wanted to know whose it was. Rav Dovid explained that the cat's services had been "enlisted" to keep the mice out of the yeshiva's storage room.

"Who feeds the cat?" asked the *rosh yeshiva*.

"Why, he eats the mice!" replied Rav Dovid Yosef.

"And what happens when there are no mice left? You just said the cat was there to keep out the mice. What if he does not get enough to eat?" The *rosh yeshiva* then got a small bowl, washed it, filled it with milk, and placed it in front of the cat. He then turned to Rav Dovid Yosef and said, "You must feed the cat every day, especially since you brought it here to do you a service!"

Elazar ben Azaria gets in the last word: Respect one another!

The new rebbe sends a note home to all the parents on the first day of school: "If you promise not to believe everything your child says happens at school, I'll promise not to believe everything he says happens at home!"

# Week 16

## On Doing What's Right — Free Will

*Do what you say, just don't talk about what you do!*
— *Yiddish folk saying*

A Jewish merchant came into the warehouse of Rav Shraga Feivel Frank, father-in-law of Rabbi Isser Zalman Meltzer, and asked for a discount in return for buying a large quantity of fur. Rav Shraga Feivel politely refused to reduce the price, explaining he wanted to make a certain profit on each skin. The merchant left the warehouse but couldn't find a better price elsewhere so he returned and told Rav Shraga he was willing to go ahead.

"I will sell you the fur, but at the discount price that you demanded."

The merchant was flabbergasted. "First you flatly refuse to give me any sort of discount and now that I'm prepared to pay, you reduce the price?"

"After you left the shop, I realized that considering your large order, I really should have given you a better price. Now that you've come back to buy from me, I must remain true to my feelings!"

# Doing What Comes Naturally!

In a very discreet manner, the Gerer Rebbe, Rav Yisroel Alter, used to help dozens of hungry families in Yerushalayim by providing them with food on a regular basis. In 1947, when the city was under siege and being shelled by Arab forces, most people didn't dare leave the bomb shelters. However, a few men, under the leadership of the Rebbe, walked the streets without a hint of fear. They were *shluchei mitzva*, "messengers sent to perform a mitzva," and were not at all concerned about being hurt themselves. When asked how he dared to send people out into the streets under such dangerous circumstances, he replied curtly, "One who fears God needn't be afraid of bombs!"

"Do what is right!" sings King David.

This requires *seichel* (common sense), known as the "fifth Shulchan Aruch," which teaches only one thing: the application of Torah and mitzvos to real life is based on sanity and reasonableness, on doing the right thing (*seichel* is the Yiddish derivation of *sevara*, a rabbinic term from the Aramaic root *sevar*, "to think").

If it's common sense, concludes Rabbi Ashi of Babylon, it needs no scriptural proof and has the full force of Jewish law.

Preparing the Jews for their entrée into the Holy Land, Moshe warns, "You will not do then as you do now, each doing what is right in his own eyes." In other words, the chaos of the desert is not going to apply to civilized society.

The phrase *do the right thing* appears earlier in the Torah, but there, *hayashar b'einav* literally means doing "what is right in His eyes [not in *yours*!]."

In Moshe's famous phrase, "Look here (*re'eh*), I place (*nosein*) before you today a blessing and a curse," the term used (*nosein*) is present, not past tense (*nasan*), which would have been more appropriate because Moshe received this law previously.

The Vilna Gaon explains the phrasing by pointing out that free will is a *daily* occurrence, happening *every moment*, and the ability to change course and do the right thing is immediate!

The Torah does another switch: it goes from the singular verb *re'eh* to *lifneichem*, which is plural. Again, the Vilna Gaon comes to the rescue: don't justify your behavior by saying everyone else is doing it. The singular tense is on purpose; each Jew is responsible for his own acts and his choice stands independently of how others behave.

> Following the terrible fire that spread across Brisk in 1895, Reb Chaim Soloveitchik worked tirelessly, day and night, to help the homeless find places to live. During that time, Reb Chaim did not sleep at home but on the ramp outside the *shul*. People pleaded with him to go home and get a good night's sleep in his own bed, but he said, "You don't understand. It doesn't feel right. I can't bring myself to sleep in my bed when I know that there are so many Jews who don't have a roof over their heads."

Commenting on the Torah verse "Let us make Man in Our image (*tzelem*), after Our likeness (*demus*)," the Rambam explains that these descriptive terms (*tzelem*, *demus*) are not physical but intellectual.

In other words, God has given man the intelligence to choose what to believe in and then to make an intelligent choice to do the right thing.

> It was Friday evening and the *Chofetz Chaim* came home from *shul* with several poor guests. But instead of singing *Shalom Aleichem*, the welcoming of the pre-Shabbas angels of peace, the *Chofetz Chaim* made Kiddush, ate, and only then sang the tune. When asked why, he explained, "I knew that the poor men I had invited were very hungry and were eager to eat, but *die malachim zeinen doch nisht hungerig un kennen varten*, the angels weren't hungry and could wait!"

The strange response to Avraham rushing to give three guests water and food was "*Ken ta'aseh ka'asher dibarta* (Do just as you said)." What does this mean? Rabbi Zevin, editor of the *Encyclopedia Talmudit*, explains that to act out one's good intentions takes three steps: thought, speech and action.

Often something gets lost between the thought and the act. The guest-angels were impressed that Avraham did exactly as he said he would!

The last word goes to that wise chassid who, when asked to explain the secret of his success, said, "I kept my mind awake — and my desire asleep!"

One day the neighbor looks over his fence and notices little Yossi in his back garden filling in a hole, and politely asks, "Nu, Yossi, what are you up to there?"

"My goldfish died, and I've just buried him."

"Oh, I'm sorry to hear that…but isn't that hole too big just for a goldfish?"

"No," Yossi replies, patting down the last heap of earth, "because he's inside your stupid cat!"

# Week 17

## On Flattery — The "Evil Eye"

*What begins as flattery matures into falsehood.*
— *Yiddish folk saying*

A follower of Rav Simcha Bunim, the Rebbe of Peshischa, came to the Rebbe and told him how jealous he had been that his father had been a great *tzadik* and he wasn't. However, the night before he had had a vivid dream. In the dream, the man's father appeared and told his son that the time had come for him to also become a great *tzadik*!

Throughout the dream recollection the Rebbe said nothing. When the man had finished, he asked the Rebbe, "*Nu*, so what do you think I should do?"

The Rebbe answered, "I suggest, the next time your father comes to you in a dream and tells you to become a blessed *tzadik*, ask your father to appear in the dreams of many others and tell them they should wake up and become your disciples!"

# Flattery Will Get You...Nowhere?

> Rav Chaim Kanievsky would quote the Gemora that if a person is worried that his own envy might cast an *ayin hora* (evil eye) on his friend, he should look at the left side of his own nose. Rav Eliyahu Dushintzer was once seen walking out of a beautiful wedding hall with his right eye closed. When asked why, he said the drapes in the hall were exceptionally beautiful and he was worried that looking at them would cause an *ayin hora*...so he closed his right eye to avoid staring at them.

When Yaakov blessed Ephraim and Menashe, it was to be like the fish in the sea. Out of sight, out of the public eye, away from the dangers of *ayin hora*, the "evil eye."

*Ayin hora* describes the negative results created by people looking at you with envy, ill-feeling, selfishness, grudges or jealousy.

Thus, Jews shouldn't flaunt their success nor possessions, which is an invitation to an *ayin hora*.

Jewish mystics added the popular abbreviated expression of *kein einahora* to a sentence, meaning "let there be no evil eye," whilst Jewish law promoted its opposite, *ayin tova*, a "good eye," in the spirit of generosity and goodwill, urging Jews to always see the best, not the worst, in other Jews.

And the reverse is also true: "Don't be wicked (even in your) own eyes," adds *Pirkei Avos* (i.e., too much self-criticism and humility are also unhealthy!).

But if you are a descendant of Yosef, the patriarch who resisted a Biblical seductress, you are immune. How do we know? From this invocation in the Talmud: "Take the thumb of the right hand in the left hand and the thumb of the left hand in the right hand, and say, 'I, so-and-so, am of the seed of Yosef over which the evil eye has no power!'"

> Alexander the Great once visited the Garden of Eden and was given an eyeball. He weighed it against all his gold and silver, but the eye was heavier. "Put some dust on it," he was told, and the scales tipped in favor of the eye. The lesson? The human eye is never satisfied; the more it sees the more it wants, until finally the dust covers it in the grave. Remember: it was Bilam's evil eye, together with "an arrogant spirit and greedy soul," that caused God to thwart Bilam and change his curse of the Jews into a blessing!

The Talmud lists a flatterer as one of four classes of people who will never merit to greet the *Shechina*. Eleazar ben Pedat goes one step further: "Flatterers are destined for *Gehinnom*, and will ultimately fall into the hands of those they flatter!"

Mishlei was blunt: a flattering mouth...works ruin!

Flattery to gain approval is especially despicable, and will only end in the phony flatterer "falling prey to the undeserving beneficiary and, if not to him, to his children or grandchildren!"

Philo called flattery "a diseased friendship"; the Yiddishists called it a form of theft, adding that a mirror fools none but the ugly; meanwhile, *Koheles* was its usual pessimistic self, declaring all is vanity!

> Rabbi Avraham Shmuel Sofer, author of *Ksav Sofer* and *av beis din* of Pressburg, was a man of measured words. Before speaking he calculated the issue from each angle to ensure that what he was about to do or say was both truthful and virtuous. It disturbed Rabbi Avraham terribly when someone praised him for something he had done or for a *shiur* that he had given, and he always stopped the person short. He was afraid that the man was merely trying to flatter him.

A prominent *rav* in Eretz Yisroel was once asked what he liked most about Rabbi Aryeh Levin. The *rav* replied, "Rabbi Levin has been frequenting my home for about twenty years now and, while he is always polite and appreciative, he has never tried to flatter me. Nor have I ever heard a negative word about anyone coming from his mouth!"

But some flattery is OK.

The Midrash says a husband may flatter his wife for the sake of *shalom bayis*, a man can flatter his creditor to get another chance, and a student may flatter his Rebbe if that'll get him more attention!

The final word goes to Moshe ibn Ezra: I am below what they say — but above what they think!

Stanley is reading the morning paper at the breakfast table and comes across an article about a beautiful movie star who is about to marry a football player who is known for his stupidity and low luck. He turns to his wife and says, "You know, I'll never understand why the biggest jerks get the most attractive wives."

She replies, "Why, thank you, dear!"

# Week 18

## On Fleeing Falsehood — *Emes*

> The truth is the safest lie!
> — *Yiddish folk saying*

When Rav Yaakov Kamenetsky was a student in Slabodka, he was invited to spend Pesach at the home of Rav Nosson Tzvi Finkel, the Alter of Slabodka, along with a few of his friends. While there, he was served some cookies made from matza meal which, for some reason or another, he preferred not to eat. The young Yaakov did not want to offend his hosts, so he declined, explaining that he did not eat *gebrochts* (food cooked or baked with matza meal), an explanation that was readily accepted. Up until that day, Rav Yaakov had, in fact, eaten *gebrochts*, since that was the custom in his parents' home. However, from that day onward, his excuse was the truth.

Rav Yaakov never again ate *gebrochts* on Pesach. When he married and had his own family Rav Yaakov did not expect them to follow this stringency but, as far as he was concerned, he was not prepared to go back on his word.

POSTCRIPT: When asked by others to what he attributed his longevity, Reb Yaakov would reply, "I never told a lie!"

# Liar, Liar!

> The Vizhnitzer Rebbe, Rav Yisroel Hager, concerned not to say anything that had a hint of untruth to it, would often preface his words with "It seems to me," rather than presenting his opinion in an assertive manner. Once the Rebbe had to send a letter but felt compelled to leave out a detail on account of its inaccuracy. Not wanting to send a lie, he decided to send the message via telegram because that required fewer words, and recipients understood it couldn't contain the entire message. Although this was more costly, the Rebbe thought it eliminated a lot of potential problems of absolute truthfulness.

God hates four types of people: mockers, hypocrites, slanderers — and liars! "He who engages in deceit shall not dwell within My house!"

Misleading words, described as a "work of deception," are a form of stealing known as *geneivas da'as,* or as Rav Yehuda Hachassid calls it, "cunning smooth-talking." Rav Yehuda even extends this discipline to body parts! Don't nod "yes" when it's a *no,* and vice versa!

When the *Chazon Ish* once overheard someone shouting at his friend, "You're a liar!" he turned to him and said, "You, too, are out of line. Even to say the word 'lie' is undesirable. It is preferable that you say, 'You are not speaking the truth!'"

Lies, adds the Talmud bluntly, "have no legs (to stand on)."

And worse: liars believe their own lies, and the truth when spoken by a habitual liar is still regarded as a lie! To correct one lie, adds *Shevet Yehuda,* "seven others have to be told!"

> A Jew once approached Rav Isser Zalman Meltzer and asked for a donation. Rav Isser reached into his pocket and handed him some money, saying, "This is all I have on me right now." A few hours later, he knocked on the man's door. "I'm sorry to disturb you, but after I told you that was all the money I had on me I found another coin in my pocket, so I feel obligated to keep my word." With that, he gave the surprised Jew a coin and left.

Once, after he had rendered a decision, the *Chazon Ish* decided he had made a mistake and immediately notified the litigants — two years later! "I want to hear the truth from whomever it may come," he writes. "I am not one to be stubborn because I know that man is full of mistakes!"

The Kotzker Rebbe was known as "the pillar of truth" because *emes* was on his mind at all times. "Everything in the world can be imitated except truth," he would say, "for truth that is imitated is no longer truth!"

For the Satmar Rav it was not enough to just refrain from *sheker* (lying), nor to "distance" oneself from falsehood (*mid'var sheker tirchak*); he insisted that one must always speak the *emes* (truth).

This means choosing your words so carefully as never to utter a falsehood.

> After traveling overnight Rabbi Yehuda Tzadka had missed his regular all-night *shiur*. When he finally arrived, there was still some time left before *Shacharis* so he said to a student, "Let's squeeze in a few moments of precious learning." The two sat down and began to learn but after a few minutes Rav Yehuda abruptly closed his *sefer* and said, "I must leave now. In a few moments people will begin arriving for *Shacharis*, and if they see me they will think that I spent the night in the *beis medrash* learning Torah. I cannot lead them to believe what is not true. That would be *geneivas da'as!*"

The Sforno claims it's possible to say the truth (e.g., out of context) and *still* transgress the order to flee from falsity ("Be cautious with your words, lest *they* learn to lie!"); meanwhile, the *Chofetz Chaim*, aware of the traditional *vort* that truthfulness is one of the pillars on which the world stands, extended this "truth antennae" both to words *and* thoughts!

> Rabbi Refoel of Barshad was scrupulous about speaking only the truth. When his children were infants, he would lean over their cradles and whisper to them, "*Mid'var sheker tirchak* (Distance yourself from falsehood)!" One day a student came into the house drenched from the weather and Rav Refoel asked him, "Is it raining outdoors?" The student, aware of his Rebbe's meticulousness, replied very precisely, "When we were outside it was raining!"

In general: if you add to the truth, you subtract from it!

A Hindu priest, a rabbi and a lawyer were driving down the road, when the car broke down. Fortunately they found a farmhouse nearby, but the farmer informed them that he had only one spare room, and that it had only two beds. They were welcome to it, but one of them had to sleep in the barn. After much discussion, the Hindu volunteered to go to the barn. A few moments later there was a knock on the bedroom door, and the Hindu explained that there was a cow in the barn, and cows are sacred and he could not possibly sleep in the barn with a cow.

So the rabbi volunteered. But a few moments later, he returned to say there was a pig in the barn and that he could not possibly spend the evening in the barn with the origin of pork.

Finally the lawyer volunteered to sleep in the barn. A few moments later there was a knock on the door, and in walked the cow and the pig.

# Week 19

## On Forgiveness

Anyone who understands his foolishness is already a little wiser.
— *Yiddish folk saying*

One Yom Kippur, prior to the *Ne'ila* service, a young man asked the Steipler Gaon what time he expected *Ne'ila* to conclude, but the Steipler motioned to the man that he did not know. Immediately after davening, the Steipler called for the young man and begged his forgiveness for not having answered his question more respectfully.

"When you came over to me I did not answer you properly because I had already begun *Ashrei*. However, as soon as you left, I realized that what I did was wrong, since it is permissible to interrupt a recitation of *Ashrei* in order to accord proper respect to another human being. You see, even on Yom Kippur prior to *Ne'ila* it is so easy to stumble. Please forgive me for my insolence," said the Steipler.

The Steipler would not rest until the man said "I forgive you." Then he gave the man a copy of one of his *seforim* as an expression of his sincere apology.

# To Forgive Is to Be Forgiven

> A man came to Rabbi Eliyahu Lopian asking his forgiveness for having offended him. "I don't recall you ever having offended me. How can I forgive something of which I am not aware? Please come back in two weeks. In the interval, I will study the *mussar* writings on how to overcome resentments, so that my forgiving will be wholehearted." Two weeks later the man returned. Rav Eliyahu embraced him, "I want to forgive you with all my heart, and thank you for the opportunity to improve on this important character trait!"

The ability to forgive those who have offended is a herculean task.

And the ability not to bear a grudge is a mitzva that the *Sefer Hachinuch* describes as one of the most difficult of them all, for it requires a monumental dose of humility and an unassuming nature.

To pardon, as Yosef does his brothers who sold him into slavery, instead of the more natural instinct of seeking revenge, is a sign of piety.

> A *talmid* of Rav Aaron Kotler related that one year, shortly before Rosh Hashana, his rebbe sent a telegram to another rabbi in the United States asking for his forgiveness. Rav Aaron later explained to his students that he had no recollection of ever slighting that particular rabbi. "However, recently, this rabbi [whom he did not name, of course] humiliated me in public, so I assume that I must have done something to hurt him. In that case, I need to beg his forgiveness!"

The son of Rav Chaim Palagi recalls how his father greeted everyone with a smile and when those who had offended him came to ask for forgiveness, Reb Chaim always greeted them graciously. "The person never felt as though my father was castigating him, but only that he wanted to help him as one friend helps another."

True forgiveness requires one to turn back the clock and start all over again. Forgiving and letting go of the past are flip sides to the same coin of reconciliation.

> Two chassidic rebbes were walking beside a river when they came across an elderly Jewish woman who was scared to cross over. One rebbe gently took her hand and helped her navigate the waters to the safety of the other side. The two continued walking but after several minutes the other rebbe began to rebuke his friend: "Surely that was not right what you did! It's against the Torah to touch a woman. How could you go against our commandments?" The rebbe complained on and on for hours. Finally, the other rebbe

interrupted, "Yes, I helped her across the river, but that was several hours ago! You're the one who's still carrying her!"

In his *Sefer Hanhaga*, Rabbi Asher ben Yechiel reveals that each night, before retiring, he would make a list of those who hurt him that day and forgive them, a magnanimous custom inspired by Raba's "He who forgives will himself be forgiven!"

Or as an old chassidic proverb goes: Be the master of your will, and the slave of your conscience!

The *Chofetz Chaim* held no personal resentment against anybody because he saw the "offender" as an agent of God's will.

> Rav Chaim Brim, *rosh yeshiva* of Mishkan Yosef, regularly served as a *ba'al tefilla* over the Yomim Noraim in New Square, New York. One year, just before *Kol Nidrei*, Rav Chaim began wandering among the benches asking people where a certain person sat. When he finally located him, he whispered something into his ear and then quickly took his seat. Rav Chaim was unable to enter Yom Kippur until he apologized to the man for cutting him off in the middle of speaking when he had bumped into him in Yerushalayim, two years earlier!

What if the other person isn't as magnanimous as you? After you have asked to be forgiven three times, codifies the Rambam, you're off the hook! The obligation then shifts to the one being asked for forgiveness to give it ("If the other still does not forgive, the injuring party may cease and the other is the sinner!").

Moishie becomes drunk at a *vort* and makes a fool of himself in front of his wife and family. The next day, now sober, he begs forgiveness from his wife, who accepts his apology with these words: "I'll forgive and forget!"

Nevertheless, for weeks and months, she continues to remind her husband of his past misdeed. Finally, Moishie says, "I thought you agreed to forgive and forget?"

She replies, "Yes, I did, but I didn't agree to let you forget that I agreed to forgive and forget!"

# Week 20

## On *Gemilus Chasadim*

A wise word is not a substitute for a piece of herring!
— *Yiddish folk saying*

Rav Bentzion Abba Shaul was known for his selflessness and amazing patience in helping others. One evening a relative came to pick up the *rosh yeshiva* and go out to a *simcha*. As they were leaving, the phone rang. Rav Bentzion answered the caller's question in halacha and then started to leave. As they were leaving, it rang again. Rav Bentzion went back to answer it, concerned it might be urgent. By now the relative's patience was running out. "This is impossible!" he complained, "we'll never get out of this house."

"You're right," replied the *rosh yeshiva*. "It's impossible for me to leave when I know that there might be a desperate person on the line."

"I have an idea. Next time, I'll answer the phone. If I think it's an emergency I'll hand it to you. Otherwise I'll ask the caller to phone back later in the evening."

"No!" shouted Rav Bentzion. "What about the sin of stealing? If you answer the phone in vain, you will cost the caller the price of a phone call!"

Meanwhile, the phone rang again and Rav Bentzion ran to pick it up.

# Good Deeds Are Better Than Wise Sayings

> Rav Leib Chasman, *rosh yeshiva* of Hevron, once asked a student, "Please, do me a favor. Kindly go into the kitchen and ask my rebbetzin to pour me a glass of tea." The student quickly rushed to carry out his Rebbe's wishes but before he had a chance to leave, Rav Leib asked him, "Tell me, why are you doing as I ask?" Embarrassed, the boy replied, "I wish to perform the mitzva of serving a *talmid chacham*." Rav Leib was expecting this answer, and responded, "You were about to perform an absolute case of *gemilus chasadim* by bringing an elderly man a glass of tea. Instead, you lost focus of the essence of the greater mitzva and decided to serve a *talmid chacham* — when I may not even be!"

*Gemilus chasadim* (acts of kindness) is one leg of the triangle that the world "stands on." The other two are *avoda* (service of Hashem) and Torah.

What do these three have in common?

They form the glue that holds society together; when all three act in unison, the result is a healthy set of relationships, with God (via *avoda-tefilla*), with oneself (Torah-mitzvos), and with others (*gemilus chasadim*).

Remove any one of these three relationships and the structure of societal peace and harmony is in jeopardy. And a caution! Even if they are *all* practiced faithfully we can still place communal stability at risk. How? By not knowing the priorities!

> When he was a young boy, Rav Avraham Yehoshua Heschel, the Kapishnitzer Rebbe, would go around his town every morning, before dawn, and anonymously leave food on the doorsteps of those in need so they could wake up with a sense of dignity. The Rebbe once pawned his silver Shabbas candlesticks to lend another Jew some money, content with simple metal candlesticks until he was repaid. When he was a child of six the future Rabbi Alexander Moshe Lapidus, *av beis din* of Rassian, would give his lunch to a needy boy in his *cheder* and not eat until he got home for supper.

"I desire kindness [among people]," God advises, "not sacrifice [to Me]," a startling subordination that even defers the study of Torah to *gemilus chasadim*.

And so Eliezer, looking for a suitable *shidduch* for Avraham's son, chooses Rivka, not based on any display on her part of *avoda* or Torah, but on a single act of *chesed*: she offers his camels a drink!

Rav Shlomo Zalman Auerbach, having derived the word *gemul* from "payment," believed that kindness received is "payment" for kindness given.

> It was suggested to Rav Eliyahu Chaim Meisels that he spend more time learning Torah and less time in community affairs. Rav Chaim Brisker answered on behalf of his friend, "The Gemora of a *rav* who closes it in order to involve himself in *tzedaka* and *chesed*, in reality is always open, while the Gemora of a *rav* who decides to ignore his responsibilities towards *klal Yisrael* and chooses not to close it, in reality is always shut!"

A startling Gemora has this to say: "Any bride with nice eyes, one doesn't have to check anymore for blemishes."

This seems to be a direct contradiction of the traditional view of beauty, as articulated in *Mishlei*'s *Eishes Chayil*, traditionally sung on Shabbas night: "*Isha yiras Hashem hi sis'halal* (A woman who fears *Hashem* should be praised)."

The *Kli Yakar* explains: to "look at the eyes" is a metaphor to see how one looks *at others*! When the bride looks to interact with others through the prism of concern, compassion and doing good deeds, it's a sign that in her DNA makeup is...*gemilus chesed*!

> Rabbi Abbahu sent his son Chanina to study in Tiberias and found out that he was busy doing community work, so he wrote him: "My son, was there no good to be done in Caesarea, your native town, that I sent you to Tiberias? Haven't we decided that learning takes precedence?"
>
> The rabbis of Caesarea replied: "Learning comes first only if there are others to do the works of kindness; but if there is no one else, doing comes first!"

Remember: it was only *after* Moshe carried a tired sheep on his shoulders that God was convinced He had chosen the right person: "If you have such mercy on part of the flock, then you are a suitable leader for My flock, Yisroel!"

A Jew is thus distinguished through his compassion — in Hebrew, *rachmanus*, derived from *rechem* (womb), implying a motherly feeling ("As one whom his mother comforts," says Yeshayahu, "so will I [God] comfort you").

*Pirkei Avos*, the epitome of wise words, is the first to admit: Good deeds are better than wise sayings!

The rabbi was distressed at the lack of generosity among his congregants, and he prayed that the rich should give more charity to the poor.

"And has your prayer been answered?" asked his wife.

"Half of it was," replied the rabbi. "The poor are willing to accept!"

# Week 21

## On *Giving the Benefit of the Doubt*

> God may have created man before woman,
> but there is always a rough draft before the masterpiece.
>
> — *Yiddish saying*

One Tisha b'Av, Rav Levi Yitzchak of Berdichev, a Jew legendary for his inability to see evil in other Jews, noticed a Jew eating a meal. He approached him, and asked, "*Reb Yid*, perhaps you have forgotten that today is Tisha b'Av?"

"No, rabbi, I know quite well that today is the ninth of Av."

"Then, *Reb Yid*, perhaps you do not know that Tisha b'Av is a fast day?"

"No, rabbi, I know quite well."

"If so, then you must not be feeling well and the doctors have probably forbidden you to fast?"

"No, rabbi, thank God, I'm in great shape and perfectly healthy."

Rav Levi Yitzchak lifted his eyes heavenwards, and said, "*Ribbono shel Olam*, look with a favorable Eye at how carefully Your children try to adhere to the mitzva of *emes*. This Jew chose to incriminate himself and make himself look like a *rasha*, rather than lie about the truth!"

# Seeing Is Not Believing!

Rav Yosef Chaim Sonnenfeld of Yerushalayim was once asked, "If you saw a bareheaded Jew walking together with a sinner on Yom Kippur, eating forbidden foods and smoking a cigarette, what would you say in his defense?"

"I could say that the man is bareheaded for health reasons and that he is eating the food and smoking because his life depends on these things. He is walking together with a sinner because he is blind and needs the man to lead him. Even if he is not blind, perhaps he is dizzy and needs help walking!"

When judging other Jews, if you have to be definitive, always make it a definite *maybe*!

The moment man was created "upright" in God's image the preservation of human dignity (*kavod habriyos*) became a desirable character trait.

Once, at a medical examination, Rav Nosson Tzvi Finkel, totally absorbed in the dignity of the other, thought it was too disrespectful to stick out his tongue when asked.

Responsible Jewish leaders stand out from the others because they always praised the nation's goodness, not its faults; "*V'shoftu es ha'am mishpat tzedek* (They shall judge the people with righteous judgment)."

Both Eliyahu Hanavi and Yeshayahu were punished for their negative comments.

This is why God chose an obscure Gideon ben Yoash to lead the nation, urging him to "go with this strength of yours!" What strength? Gideon acted in accord with the twin orders in the Mishna, "Judge everyone favorably," and "Refrain from judging until you are in their situation."

When Shlomo Carlebach went to Russia he would take with him many pairs of tefillin and yarmulkes for the refuseniks. Once on the last day of his trip, a twelve-year-old boy knocked on his door and asked if he could have a pair of tefillin. Reb Shlomo said he was very sorry, but he had already given away his last pair. The boy began to cry bitterly. So Reb Shlomo gave him his own pair, which he had inherited from his father and had precious sentimental value. The boy thanked Reb Shlomo, and asked if he could also have a yarmulke. Reb Shlomo took off the yarmulke from his head and gave it to the boy. At the airport the next morning, on his way back from Russia, Shlomo asked another Jew if he could borrow his tefillin. The Jew looked at

> him and said, "Hey, before you worry about tefillin, why don't you start wearing a yarmulke!"

The safest course, adds Philo, first-century Jewish thinker, is to always suspend judgment!

Only the arrogant, adds Shmuel Uceda in his *Sefer Midrash Shmuel*, don't doubt; and "at every moment," urged the great chassidic rabbi, Elimelech of Lizhensk, "every Jew must only see the *ma'alos* (positive attributes) of every other Jew, and never see their *chesronos* (shortcomings)!"

> When Rav Yosef Shaul Natanson of Lvov, author of *Shoel u'Meishiv*, dropped in to visit Rav Meir'l of Premishlan for the first time, he was shocked to see the elderly *gadol* sitting at a table bare of *seforim*, staring into space. He had expected to see the *tzadik* poring over multiple *seforim*. Rav Meir sensed the disappointment and politely rebuked the younger *rav* for not being disciplined to always judge other Jews favorably (in fact, Rav Meir was deep in the Bobov custom of doing *teshuva* in preparation for Torah study, which required no distractions).

Whenever he saw a car driving in Jerusalem on Shabbas, Rav Aharon Rokeach, the Belzer Rebbe, would comment, "There are so many Arabs in Yerushalayim!" When told a certain Jew didn't put on tefillin, the Rebbe replied, "You mean Rabbeinu Tam's tefillin!"

To show respect to another, explains Rav Yeruchem, the Mirrer *mashgiach*, is derived from the belief that every person is created in the image of God.

The scene of a Jew knee-deep in the mud is famous: did he fall in, or does he want to be there?

Not only must he be given the benefit of the doubt but, urges Rabbi Solomon ben Meir Halevi of Karlin, "If what you want is to help someone rise from the mud and filth, don't think it's enough to stand on top and offer a hand by reaching down. You must go down yourself, down into the mud and filth itself. Then take the person with your strong grip and pull both of you out into the light!"

Moishie, fresh out of accounting school, shows up at an interview and is asked, "What's three times seven?"

"Twenty-two," Moishie replies.

When he gets home he double-checks his answer on his calculator and realizes he's not going to get the job.

A few weeks later, he is shocked to receive a letter offering him the job! When he shows up on his first day at work, Moishie asks his boss how he got the job, considering he got such a simple question wrong.

"Well," shrugs the boss, "you were the closest!"

# Week 22

## Gone Fishing!

A vacation is what you take when you can no longer
take what you've been taking!

— *Yiddish folk saying*

One day Rav Shimshon Raphael Hirsch closed his Talmud and told his students he was leaving to go hiking in the Alps for three days. The students were shocked that their holy *rav* was going on vacation. "Someday," Rav Hirsch explained to his incredulous *talmidim*, "I shall come before the Almighty, and He may ask me, '*Nu*, Shimshon, so what do you think of My Alps?' and I must be ready to tell Him, 'They are magnificent!'"

So put this book down, pack your bags, and take your wife away on a week's vacation.

See you next week!

# Week 23

## On Greeting with a Smile

Guests and rain are the same; if they stay long they are a nuisance. Just hide the misfortunes beneath a smile!

— *Yiddish folk saying*

Rav Nosson Tzvi Finkel, the Alter of Slabodka, always invited *meshulachim* into his home and gave them not only a donation but good cheer and emotional support as well. Despite his physical pain, Rav Nochum Perchovitz, *rosh yeshiva* of Mir, would greet everyone he met with great joy and warmth, explaining, "A person's face is like public property, and is visible to all. Therefore, one may not allow his facial expression to be a 'pit in public property.'"

In other words, his expression should not become a source of pain for others.

When Rav Eliyahu Dessler saw one of his pupils walking around with a long face, he said, "You are like a thief! What right do you have to deprive your fellow human beings of the pleasantness of a cheerful face?"

# Smile...and the World Smiles with You!

> Rav Moshe Porush once sent a number of rabbis to try to convince a young *yeshiva bochur* to return to learning, but to no avail. He then asked Rav Yehuda Tzadka, *rosh yeshiva* of *Porat Yosef,* to see the boy. Amazingly, after a relatively brief conversation, the boy agreed to go back to the yeshiva and ultimately grew into a wonderful *ben Torah*. "All the other rabbis," he explained years later, "warned me harshly what would happen to me if I left the yeshiva. But *Chacham Yehuda* smiled and empathized with me. He convinced me that, in the long run, I would be much happier and better off learning Torah. His smile conquered me and I could not refuse him!"

There's a puzzling expression, *U'leven shinayim mei'chalav,* which on the surface translates as "white-toothed from milk."

But, explains Reb Yochanan, it can also be read as *libun shinayim,* "whitening one's teeth," in that offering someone an (uplifting) "white smile" can sometimes be more virtuous than offering them a glass of milk!

The Maharal elaborates: a physical donation (milk, money, etc.) to the poor is only a temporary relief, but a warm smile can uplift the spirit and sustain one's emotions. "Someone who gives a coin to the poor will be blessed with six blessings, whereas the one who addresses him with words of comfort will be blessed with eleven blessings — *even* if he does *not* give him a donation!"

> Like so many *gedolim*, the *Chazon Ish* was extremely gracious to everyone he met. When a small child wished him a *gut Shabbas*, he would return the courtesy with a wide smile and with great respect as if he were responding to a very important person. He was so warm and friendly that some children pranksters would run towards him just to shout "hello" because they knew he would always respond. And they were right: the *Chazon Ish* always smiled and returned the "courtesy."

The *Chazon Ish* wore glasses for shortsightedness outdoors, but never in the *beis medrash*. Why? He wanted to be able to see clearly if someone was approaching so he could acknowledge his greeting.

It's easy, writes Rav Shlomo Wolbe in his *sefer Alei Shor*, "to greet friends and relatives with a smile," but it's more important to be gracious to "strangers and beggars." Friends and relatives you see all the time; strangers and beggars you may never bump into again.

And so the Ramban urged discipline: "Accustom yourself to greet people gently at all times."

Shammai had a reputation for being strict and stern, yet was warm in his greetings ("Receive everyone with a cheerful face," he urged), as was Rabbi Yochanan ben Zakai, who always greeted another first.

> Rabbi Shlomo Wolbe told of a non-religious Jew who walked through a chareidi neighborhood every day on his way to work. After a while, the neighborhood noticed a change in the way he dressed, and then, one day, they noticed that he had grown *peyos*. When asked what had inspired him to become a *ba'al teshuva*, he explained that during the years he walked through the neighborhood one chareidi Jew always greeted him warmly every day, and wished him well.
>
> "I began to think more deeply about the differences in our lifestyles," he explained, "and I slowly became more and more drawn to the beauty of *yiddishkeit*."

Since it is an obligation to make others feel good, smiling is catching, happiness contagious. Others mirror what they see: a frown is never met with a smile ("As water reflects one's face, so too the human heart reflects the heart of another!").

The epitome of a Jew who always responded to events with a smile and an optimistic sigh was Nachum Ish Gam-Zu, a sage of the Mishna so named for his habit of saying "*Gam zu l'tova* (This also is for the best!)" Rabbi Akiva said the same; his response to being robbed was, "Everything God does is for the best."

Jews, wanting to know that God is happy with them, ask for a sign of a happy Divine Face ("Illuminate Your Face that we may be saved!").

Reb Simcha Zissel of Kelm adds that it's a matter of habit: if you discipline yourself to be polite, smiling, friendly and well mannered to everybody, then being courteous to God will come naturally!

The always friendly Tom is applying for a job as a signalman for the local railroad and is told to meet the inspector at the signal box.

The inspector decides to give Tom a pop quiz, asking, "What would you do if you realized that two trains were heading towards each other on the same track?"

The smiling Tom says, "I would switch one train to another track."

"What if the lever broke?" asks the inspector.

"Then I'd run down to the tracks and use the manual lever down there," answers Tom.

"What if that had been struck by lightning?" challenges the inspector.

"Then," Tom continued, "I'd run back up here and use the phone to call the next signal box."

"What if the phone was busy?"

"In that case," Tom argued, "I'd run to the street level and use the public phone near the station."

"What if that had been vandalized?"

"Oh, well," says Tom, breaking out into a big smile, "in that case I would run into town and get my Uncle Leo."

"Why," asks the puzzled inspector, "would you do that?"

"Because he's never seen a train crash!"

# Week 24

## On *Hachnasas Kalla*, Sharing in *Simchas*

At every *simcha* there are two kinds of people: those who want to go home and those who don't. They're usually married to each other!

— *Yiddish folk saying*

A taxi once pulled up at the home of a bar mitzva boy and Rav Moshe Aaron Stern was shocked to see Rav Chaim Shmulevitz, then quite elderly, get out. Rav Chaim had earlier delivered a *shiur* and, drained of energy, was now straining himself even further to attend.

"Why must you exert yourself to come out in this weather to the bar mitzva? I'm sure the family would understand if you did not come," Rav Stern remarked.

"I have come because I have *hakoras hatov* to the boy's father for attending my *shmuessen*."

"What's so special about that? People are always eager to come and hear you speak. There is hardly standing room in the *beis medrash* during your *shmuessen*. If anything, you are doing him the favor."

"That may be. However, if he were not to come, and nor were the next and the next, then to whom would I speak — the walls? Therefore I must appreciate each and every individual who attends my *shmuessen*, and for this I have come to the bar mitzva."

# Simcha Blues

> Upon being invited to a bar mitzva Rav Shlomo Zalman Auerbach apologized to the father that he had two prior engagements that evening and that, regrettably, he would not be able to attend. However, Rav Shlomo surprised the family by actually showing up, explaining, "I realized that I had been to both previous bar mitzvos in the family and was afraid that if I missed this *simcha*, the bar mitzva boy would be upset."

Physically sharing in other people's joy is a fulfillment of the premiere mitzva to show love for a fellow Jew. And there's a selfish reason: if you pour happiness on others, it's inevitable that you'll spill a few drops on yourself!

There are three parts to the mitzva of *hachnasas kallah*: bring a girl to the *chuppa*, bring joy to the *chasan* and *kalla* (which the Tur claims is a *mitzva gedola*, a "great mitzva!"), and supply whatever needs are necessary to help the couple.

The Gemora reminds us that even Torah learning is suspended in order to bring a Jewish girl to the *chuppa*. And, reminds Rav Shlomo Zalman Auerbach, you can't leave a *chuppa* to *daven Mincha*, even if you miss the *zeman* — because you're in the middle of a mitzva!

Since "one who gladdens a bridegroom is privileged to acquire knowledge of the Torah," Rabbi Samuel, despite his age and infirmity, would dance in front of the bride whilst juggling three myrtle twigs (reminiscent of Rabban Shimon ben Gamliel's expert juggling of eight torches at the *simchos beis hasho'eva*).

Some of his rabbinic colleagues said he was brilliant, others called his antics foolish. But when he died, a pillar of fire appeared in front of his grave, a supernatural *siman* given only to the greatest of the generation.

*"Those who sing in the present world,"* writes Joshua ben Levi, *"will also sing in the next!"*

*Don't knock "a mere clown,"* warns the Talmud. *"He may be the first in God's heaven, if he has helped to diminish the sadness of human life."*

And so Rav Itzel Peterburger, disregarding his own humility, would enthusiastically dance at weddings as though he himself were getting married, standing on tables and singing witty *grammen* to bring laughter to the *chasan* and *kalla*.

> When Rav Yitzchak Blazer's friend, Reb Naftoli Amsterdam, married his second wife in Yerushalayim, Rav Yitzchak danced on top of a table and sang special songs to make the septuagenarian couple smile. "Why all the playfulness?" he was asked. For after all, "they are not youngsters." Rav Yitzchak replied, "I have not found any distinction between couples in their

teens and those in their seventies with regard to the mitzva of *simchas chasan v'kalla!*"

The duty of *hachnasas kalla*, "helping a bride and groom," explains Rabbi Eliezer, is a two-part mitzva: financial (providing the means of marriage and immediate other needs) and emotional (providing moral support).

Reb Eliezer says that one should care for a bride and groom as though receiving the Torah at *Har Sinai*. Rashi interprets the word *k'chaloso*, from "*Vayitein el Moshe k'chaloso l'daber ito b'Har Sinai* (When He finished speaking to him on Har Sinai, *Shemos* 31:18)," as *k'kalaso*, "like his bride!"

Noting that *kiddushin*, "betrothal," is derived from the verse "God said to Moshe *vekiddashtan* (and sanctify them)," the Tashbatz teaches that *Klal Yisroel* received the Torah in the same way a groom greets his bride (remember: all wedding customs are derived from that day of revelation on Har Sinai; for example, since the Torah begins with the letter *beis*, so does the *kesuba*).

> A father was once embarrassed to raise money for his daughter's wedding and asked a friend to do so anonymously. However, people would have given had they known who the family was but wouldn't give as much to "anonymous." So the friend asked his *rosh yeshiva*, Rav Yaakov Ruderman from Ner Israel, Baltimore, what to do: should he mention the name and get more money or keep it anonymous and get less money? Rav Ruderman replied instantly, "*A mensch's kavod iz vert a sach* (A person's pride is worth a lot)!" In other words, keep it anonymous!

Because of the embarrassment and pride involved, the *Chofetz Chaim*, in his *sefer Ahavas Chesed*, encourages communities to set up a special *hachnasas kalla* fund, confidential and dignified, and *paskened* that the mitzva of this *chesed* is not restricted to the newlywed couple, but also to the parents whose anxiety to see their children finally settled is eased by the help.

At her first *chasuna*, a little girl starts tugging at her mother's dress. "Yes *ziessaleh*, what is it?"

"How come the *kalla* looks so happy and is smiling and is all dressed in white?"

"Because white is the color of happiness, and today is the happiest day of her life."

The little girl thinks for a few minutes, and tugs at her mother's dress again.

"Yes?"

"Then how come the *chasan* is dressed in black?"

# Week 25

## On *Hachnasas Orchim*

When you feed strangers you occasionally feed angels.
— *Yiddish folk saying*

A group of people showed up for a meal at the home of Rav Yosef Shlomo Kahaneman, the Ponivezher Rav, on the wrong day. When they realized their mistake they began to apologize for intruding. Embarrassed, they explained their error and they turned around to leave.

"Oh, no!" cried Rav Kahaneman. "You have no idea how good it is that you are here now. Hosting guests after preparing for their arrival is no big deal. Real *hachnasas orchim* is receiving people who come without warning. I'm so glad that you came because now I will see if I can fulfill the mitzva in its truest sense. Thank you, and please come inside."

# It's Not Enough to Just Open the Door!

> A man had just arrived in Brisk and was schlepping his heavy bags down the main street. He stopped a Jew to ask for directions but instead the man insisted on carrying his bags. Upon arrival, the visitor thanked him profusely for his help. Later that day, he was shocked to discover the man was Rav Chaim Soloveitchik. He immediately rushed to Rav Chaim's house to apologize for having troubled the great rabbi. "I don't understand why you are apologizing," replied Rav Chaim. "You did me a huge favor by granting me the opportunity to fulfill the mitzva of welcoming a guest, and for this I am very grateful to you."

From the moment Avraham made God wait while he rushed "in the heat of the day" and in great pain following his circumcision to greet his guests, the mitzva of *hachnasas orchim* (hospitality) assumed a level of extraordinary importance.

And it wasn't enough to just open the door!

The *Chofetz Chaim* lays out the rules: guests must be greeted amicably, be immediately offered something to eat and drink (in case they're too shy to ask), and even have their emotional needs met with comforting words and blessings.

The order "You shall slice your bread for the hungry" implies that it's not enough to give your guests bread and a knife; *you* must also slice it for them! Those who feed the hungry, reminds *agadas Shir Hashirim*, "also feed God"!

And even if you do all this one hundred percent by the book and then make your guest feel uncomfortable — you've lost the mitzva!

> Whenever Rav Refoel Baruch Toledano heard that there was a guest in the city, he went to find him and be the first to extend an invitation. Rav Refoel Baruch always served his guests personally rather than rely on others to do so. In the middle of the night he would check on them to make sure they were okay and had everything they needed.

You shouldn't ask a guest for a *d'var Torah* unless you're sure he has something to say, to avoid potential embarrassment; and if your guest is sharing a Torah thought with you, don't argue with him *even* if he's wrong, so as not to cause any discomfort. If a guest arrives just as you are running out the door to learn Torah, the *Chofetz Chaim* says stay home and take care of your guest first!

What about running to catch a *minyan* to *daven*?

If your guest will feel slighted, *paskens* Rav Shlomo Zalman Auerbach, you need to *daven* later and take care of his needs first. Why? Because, explains the *Chofetz*

*Chaim*, "It does not say anywhere in the Torah to invite your guest to pray; but the Torah does require us to offer food, drink and a bed."

> Whilst passing through Yerushalayim a Jew dropped in to visit the Klausenberger Rebbe, Rav Yekusiel Yehuda Halberstam. Seeing his visitor, the Rebbe immediately went to prepare a bed for him. "No, no, that's unnecessary," said the guest. "I have a room at the hotel."
>
> "I don't believe it!" cried the Rebbe, "Such a wonderful mitzva comes my way and you want to deprive me of it?"

When Avraham plants a tamarisk tree the Hebrew used is *eshel*, an acrostic for *alef* (*ochel*, "food"), *shin* (*shtiah*, "drink") and *lamed* (*leviya/lina*, "escort/sleeping accommodations"), implying that the patriarch purposefully established a bed-and-board inn for travelers.

Avraham, the first *mensch*, did more than just greet his guests properly, he also said *good-bye* properly by *seeing his guests out*.

As a young student in Slabodka, Rav Aaron Kotler recalls how the *rosh yeshiva*, Rav Nosson Tzvi Finkel, always walked him part of the way from the *beis medrash* to his dormitory room late at night.

> Rabbi Yehuda Tzadka knew that the proper fulfillment of a mitzva is dependent on its conclusion so he insisted on personally escorting his guests out of his house. Even when he was very weak, Rav Yehuda made it a point to walk at least two or three steps out the door. When that was no longer possible, he instructed one of his children to do so!

How a guest *leaves* your home is more of a defining moment of his visit than how he arrives.

And it's psychological: if a guest leaves in a good mood he is more able to deal with obstacles in his way, accompanied, reminds *Me'am Loez*, by the *Shechina* (God's Presence), which protects him from danger.

After dinner one evening, the host decides to entertain his houseguest by playing the piano. At one point he turns to his visitor and says, "I understand you love music."

"Oh, yes, very much so," the guest responds politely. "But don't worry about it, just keep on playing…"

# Week 26

## On Harming Another — Friends and Enemies

Those who have no money to lend to friends make no enemies!
— *Yiddish saying*

A few days before Sukkos, Rav Yisroel Yaakov Kanievsky, the Steipler, went to a local *arba minim* dealer to look for a *lulav*. The Steipler looked at quite a few *lulavim* but could not find any to his liking, so he left the store. However, not five steps out the door, the Steipler turned around and went back inside. He carefully looked over the *lulavim* a second time, went on to choose one, paid for it and left. On the way home, the Steipler explained to the family member escorting him that, upon leaving the store, he realized that had he not purchased a *lulav*, a rumor would have circulated stating that the Steipler had been in the store and had not found a single *lulav* that met his standards. In such a case the proprietor would have endured a tremendous loss, so the Steipler went back and bought a *lulav* after all.

# With a Little Help from My Friends

> "The gazelle is the animal most loved by God. He sends herbs to heal her. He helps her find water in the deep pit. He gives her courage. Why does God love her? Because the gazelle harms no one, and never disturbs the peace!"
>
> — Rabbi Levi, in the name of Rabbi Shimon ben Lakish (*Midrash Rabba*)

That all of Israel is responsible for one another is an appeal for unity which, in reverse, condemns harming one another.

By holding the community responsible for certain acts of an individual, the Torah reinforces the dependence each Jew has on the other. Rabbi Yehuda even suggests that the *kehilla* is responsible for one's private acts!

Immediately following the Ten Commandments, in its delineation of the laws of injury, the Torah discusses freeing slaves *before* the sin of murder. The Rambam explains why: the primary sources of violence are such offenses as disrespect and ill treatment of those in a position of servitude.

This creates an atmosphere where the powerful exploit the weak, harass the poor and aggravate the foreigner. In this climate, the fear of God has been swept aside by the fear of man.

> "To do evil to another human being is worse than to do evil toward God," explains the Amshinover Rebbe. "The person you hurt may leave and go to a place you do not know or are incapable of reaching. Therefore you will not have the opportunity to ask to be forgiven for what you have done. God, however, so completely surrounds us with His presence that it is always possible to find him if you are truly seeking!"

The Jew who raises a hand to strike a fellow Jew is called a *rasha*, "wicked," even if he doesn't actually hit him!

When Moshe sees two Jews fighting, he doesn't accuse nor threaten, and asks not "Why *did* you hit him?" but "Why *would* you?"

The *Rama* disqualified the testimony in the *beis din* of any Jew who had degraded another Jew by hitting him. In Radin, the *Chofetz Chaim* excommunicated anyone found raising a hand against a fellow Jew. King David sang that only "one with clean hands" (i.e., who had never committed violence against another Jew) was capable of "ascending the mountain of God"!

> One evening, Rav Avraham of Porisov spent the entire night in the *beis medrash* learning Torah. The next morning, his disciples were surprised to discover how their rebbe had spent the night. "We know that you are an assiduous learner," they said, "but the entire night in the *beis medrash* is unusual!"
>
> "Unusual?" replied Rav Avraham. "Not exactly. Last night an elderly man fell asleep beside me while sitting on the bottom of my jacket. I couldn't bring myself to leave lest I wake him up!"

The prohibition known as "*V'lo sonu ish es amiso* (Do not aggrieve one another)" also applies to damaging business dealings (*onas mamon*) and hurtful speech (*onas d'varim*). Regarding financial loss, the prohibition applies not just to blatant theft but also to giving bad advice (which is why the *Chofetz Chaim* said you have to study the laws of *choshen mishpat* before you go into business); hurtful speech includes harmful advice, teasing, etc.

The *Sefer Hachinuch* says the second is worse than the first because words hurt, in that they "cause people severe anguish."

> The *rosh yeshiva* of Radin, Rav Moshe Landinsky, once asked Rav Elchonon Wasserman to knock on his door when it came time to recite *kiddush levana*. But when Reb Elchonon went to call Rav Moshe he found him dozing at his desk and didn't know what to do. Just then the *Chofetz Chaim* passed by so he asked him, "Rav Moshe told me to call him for *kiddush levana*, but now he's sleeping. What should I do?"
>
> The *Chofetz Chaim*, surprised, replied, "How can you even entertain the idea of waking up a sleeping person?"

"Even one enemy is one too many," warns Asher ben Yechiel. *Avos d'Rabbi Nosson* defines a hero as one who turns an enemy into a friend.

The Torah is crystal clear: warm feelings towards others are a must. Remember: folks are not as good as their friends represent them, nor are they are bad as their enemies depict them!

A man without friends, sighs ibn Gabirol, is like the left without the right! The Talmud's Choni Hame'agel was much more emotional: "Give me comradeship…or give me death!"

An Arab sheik finds himself sitting next to an orthodox Jew on a flight. He gets very agitated and calls the cabin attendant over to complain about his seat.

"What seems to be the problem, Sir?" asks the attendant.

"Can't you see?" he loudly snaps. "You've sat me next to a Jew. I can't possibly sit next to this disgusting man. Find me another seat!"

"Please try to be calm, Sir. I believe the economy section is completely full today, but I'll go and check to see if we have any upgraded seats available in first class."

Minutes later the stewardess returns. "Sir, as I suspected, the economy class is full but we do have one empty seat in first class. I had to get special permission from the captain but, given the extreme circumstances, he agreed that it was outrageous for one of our passengers to have to sit next to such an obnoxious person."

She then turns to the Jew and says, "So if you'd like to get your things, Sir, I have your first-class seat ready for you!"

# Week 27

## On Honoring Parents

You don't know how much you don't know until your
children grow up and tell you how much you don't know!
(Or: "Eggs think they are smarter than hens!")

— *Yiddish folk saying*

A man once went to Rabbi Chaim Brisker to ask him what he should do about visiting his sick father. On the one hand, he certainly felt it was his duty to travel abroad to visit him. At the same time, however, the halacha is that the expenses involved in honoring a parent are incumbent on the parent, not the child. Therefore, the man asked Reb Chaim if he was obligated to spend the money on a train ticket.

Reb Chaim's answer was short and concise: "No, you needn't spend a cent; walk!"

# Parents? Partners in Creation!

> Traveling by train from Warsaw to his father-in-law's home in Biala, the Gerer Rebbe sat opposite a Jewish man who stared at Reb Avraham Mordechai Alter sitting engrossed in his learning throughout the long journey.
>
> "I could not take my eyes off him," the man recalls, "and then, the Rebbe looked at his pocket watch and mumbled to himself, 'Oh, no, it's almost *tzeis hakochavim* (when three stars are visible in the sky, literally "the going out of the stars")!' Then he took out some meat sandwiches, washed his hands and quickly ate the sandwiches. I could not make sense of this. Why eat at such a late hour and why so quickly? The Rebbe explained, "The truth is I'm not hungry at all. However, this morning my mother packed me these sandwiches and told me to eat them all today. The day is almost over, so I had to eat quickly!"

Yehuda Hanasi equates honoring parents (*kabed es avicha v'es imecha*) with honoring God, but Shimon bar Yochai says it's even *greater* than honoring God!

The *Zohar* makes God, father and mother equal co-partners in Creation, and identifies the "lights of Heaven" as our parents — the father as sun, the mother as moon.

The Rambam even makes it a hereditary trait: if you don't respect your parents, your children will not respect you! The Talmud summarizes it thus: when you teach your son, you teach your son's son!

The importance of this mitzva is indicated in the fact that the rare exception where one is allowed to become a charity case and a burden on the community through excessive giving of one's own resources is if it's necessary in order to support one's parents.

When the blind Rav Yosef heard his mother's footsteps, he would quickly rise "in honor of the *Shechina* that is approaching" (God could not be everywhere — so He created mothers!), and although "I served my father my entire life," Rabbi Shimon ben Gamliel complained that "I didn't serve him even a hundredth of the way Esav treated his father [because, unlike I, he was] dressed in royal garments!"

> Rav Tarfon's mother was walking in her yard one Shabbas when a strip of her sandal was torn. Rav Tarfon stooped, placed his palms under her feet, and helped her back to bed. When he later fell ill, his mother told his visiting colleagues, "Pray for Rav Tarfon my son; he respects me even too much."

> "What did he do for you?"
> She told them. Said they, "Even if he did so a thousand times, he would not have fulfilled even half of the honor requirements of the Torah in the field of honoring parents!"

Rabbi Chaim Palagi, quoting the episode where an angel tells Gideon after an act of *kibud av*, "You are worthy of bringing about the nation's salvation!" explains that this direct Torah mitzva *alone* is worthy of bringing redemption.

And so the Manchester Gaon, Rav Yehuda Zev Segal, seeking to participate in this important mitzva, would encourage his *yeshiva bochurim* to send letters to their parents and then he would personally deliver them to the post office.

One day Rabbi Abbahu asked his son Rav Avimi for some water to drink. The young man brought the water, but his father had fallen asleep. Rav Avimi stood next to his father with the water the entire time until he awoke.

Shimon bar Yochai said: better to become a beggar than not help out your parents! Why? Say the Yiddishists, no matter how many children parents have, each child is the *only one* they have!

> The young Rabbi Salman Mutzapi was learning *kibud av v'eim* in *Meseches Kiddushin* with Rav Tzadka Chotzin. During the learning, Rav Tzadka asked Salman, "When your mother enters the room, do you rise in her honor?"
>
> "I wasn't about to lie to my rebbe," recalls Rabbi Salman, "so I conceded that I did rise, but not fully."
>
> Rav Tzadka then closed his Gemora, explaining, "We cannot have a situation where *halachos* are being learned but not practiced. If, by tomorrow, you have corrected your behavior, then we will continue to learn together!"

In his commentary on *Sefer Bereishis*, Rashi extends the honor of parents to grandparents, for it is the *parent* who is honored when a child honors his grandparents (if I'd known having grandchildren was so great, I would'a had 'em first!).

The final word goes to the Eastern European Jewish cynics: The best security for old age? Respect your children!

The boss called one of his employees into the office. "Rob," he said, "you've been with the company for a year now. You started off in the mail room, one week later you were promoted to a sales position, and one month after that you were promoted to district manager of the sales department. Just four short months later, you were promoted to vice-president. Now, it's time for me to retire, and I want you to take over the company. What do you say to that?"

"Thanks, Dad," said the employee.

# Week 28

## On Jealousy, Coveting

Every cat likes fish but few of them will enter the water!
— *Yiddish folk saying*

Despite his impoverishment, Rav Dovid Deutsch, author of *Ohel Dovid*, was always content with the little that he had. One day, the *Chasam Sofer* paid him a visit. Rav Dovid was in the middle of eating and when the *Chasam Sofer* saw the old wooden bowl and spoon with which he ate he could not contain his astonishment. He picked up the spoon and studied it closely in disbelief. Rav Dovid thought the *Chasam Sofer* was studying it with admiration, wishing it were his. Not wanting his guest to transgress the prohibition of "*Lo sachmod* (You shall not covet)," he turned to the *Chasam Sofer* and said, "You can have the spoon, I'm giving it to you wholeheartedly!" The *Chasam Sofer* loved telling this story since it illustrated the purity of a poor man who felt he had everything.

# Invite It Not!

> The Gerer Rebbe, Rav Avraham Mordechai Alter, had a huge Torah library of rare and valuable volumes. Whenever the Rebbe came across a new *sefer* he simply had to have it and insisted on paying full price. He never accepted a *sefer* as a gift, not even from the author. One day the Rebbe was visiting Rav Kalman Poppenheim in Vienna, and, as was his custom, browsed through his host's collection of *seforim*. One caught his eye. "This *sefer* is very special," the Rebbe commented, "I don't even have a copy of it!" Rav Kalman immediately jumped at the opportunity to give a gift to the Gerer Rebbe, but the Rebbe refused, explaining that "the *inyan* against jealousy is also applicable to *seforim*!"

"If a man cannot get what he wants," advises Rav Yaakov Anatoli, "he should want what he can get!"

The higher a person's profile, explains Rashi, the more he is in danger from the *ayin hora*, a swampy pool where jealousy thrives in its ability to cause trouble.

And so the Midrash advises Jewish leaders that a low, modest profile is "the healthiest way to live," as the *siddur* includes the wish, "May it be Your will that you save me from brazen people and from (my own) brazenness!"

The Talmud asks, "Who is the strange god in man?" and then answers its own question: temptation!

*Invite it not*, is Rav's short, blunt warning.

Adds the Rambam: even if you convince someone to sell you what you wanted *for full price*, it's still a sin of coveting, because of the presence of pressure.

Meanwhile, Rabbi Eleazar Hakappar puts jealousy and ambition on an equal par: both, he says, are disruptive.

The second-century sage is referring to unbridled ambition, a philosophy of excess that the Rambam tries to moderate with his advocacy of always pursuing a "middle way." The Rambam even thinks that excessive generosity impedes one's spiritual ambition!

> Rav Shraga Feivel Frank, son-in-law of Rav Isser Zalman Meltzer, was a man of means, and when he sent his son to an out-of-town yeshiva the boy was not expected to eat *teg* (literally "days"; *essen teg* meant eating meals at different homes every day of the week, which was common practice). However, Rav Shraga Feivel insisted that his son not stand out from the other *bochurim*, in order not to stir jealousy, and also insisted on repaying the families that hosted his son over the years.

According to the Talmud, there's only one acceptable form of jealousy and that's among scholars, because it increases wisdom!

This didn't stop the *Zohar* from suggesting another acceptable context ("Love without jealousy is not true love!"), nor the Midrash from adding its own exemption: "Be jealous for My sake!" demands God, crediting the normally destructive urge of jealousy for such "goodness" as a man planting his vineyard, marrying a wife and building a house!

> The Alter of Slabodka, Rav Nosson Tzvi Finkel, was convinced that his youthful craving for cookies and candies was because he saw how the other kids enjoyed them, and felt that eating the same was a result of his "jealousy." He resolved to be a disciplined *nosher*, and for the rest of his life he rarely ate cookies or candy!

In an attempt to mitigate physical jealousy, the Mishna's Ben Zoma simply redefines richness as having nothing to do with assets and everything to do with one's mental state: "Who is rich? He who is joyful with his lot!"

"I am certain," the *Chazon Ish* once commented, "that Rav Aryeh Leib Hacohen Shain had no desire for kugel. If he had, it would have been impossible for him to write his masterpiece *Sefer Ketzos Hachoshen*!"

> The *Chofetz Chaim* said there were two types of jealousy: the (natural) desire to have what another has, and the (unnatural) jealousy that comes from wanting to deprive the other of what they have. The second is far more lethal than the first because it involves malice.

A Yiddish proverb: We want what we don't have, and what we have we do not appreciate.

To covet what belongs to another is, in some cases, sinful even if it goes no further than thinking of it! Ibn Gabirol, in his sefer *Mivchar Hapeninim*, reveals the best antidote: close your eyes!

One Midrash is blunt: bad neighbors count a man's income but not his expenses! Or as the Yiddishists would put it: He is less upset by his poverty than by your wealth!

Yankie is driving down the freeway when he spots Freddie standing in the middle of a huge field of grass, doing nothing, just standing there. He pulls the car over, gets out, walks over to Freddie and says, "Hey, what are you doing?"

"Well," Freddie replies, "I've always wanted to be a Nobel Prize winner."

"So, what are you doing out here?"

"Well, I heard they give the Nobel Prize to people who are out standing in their field!"

# Week 29

## On Leadership, Fundraising

*A real leader always faces the music,
even when he doesn't like the tune!*

— *Yiddish folk saying*

On his way to his daughter's wedding in Bialystok, Rav Yisroel Salanter stopped off in the city of Lomzeh to meet with leading members of the community to discuss the *kehilla*'s dissatisfaction with their *rav*, Rabbi Yehoshua Leib Diskin.

"He has no respect for the wealthy people of the community, only for the *melamdim*, and he spends all his time learning and takes no interest in the needs of the community. What do you think we should do?"

"What do you propose?" asked Rav Yisroel.

"Well, we are prepared to give him a nice severance package and find him a new position in another city," said the president, "and then everything should be fine!"

"I will consider the matter and give you an answer tomorrow," Rav Yisroel replied.

The next day they all gathered to hear the decision.

"Look," said Rav Yisroel, "dismissing a rabbi is not a simple thing. The Midrash teaches us that when a *tzadik* leaves a city, the city's glory and splendor leave with him. Besides, most of the city's residents are very happy with their rabbi and do not wish to see him go. Therefore, it wouldn't be right to upset the majority because of a few wealthy individuals. Since the disagreement is limited to just a few people, I suggest you raise a nice severance package and give it to those wealthy individuals and, if they go, then 'everything should be fine!'"

# Appearances Matter

> When Rav Yechezkel Shinover's rebbe fell gravely ill and needed money for medical expenses, Rav Yechezkel asked his father if he could go door-to-door to raise the money. "It's fine with me," said his father, Reb Chaim Sanzer, "but only on the condition that you don't return filled with hatred of your fellow Jews."
>
> "Why should that happen?" asked Yechezkel in surprise.
>
> "Some people," Reb Chaim explained, "will refuse to give at all and others will not give as much as you would have liked. I don't want you to develop negative feelings toward them for, in such a case, you will come home with hatred instead of money. You can go as long as you promise to continue loving every single Jew!"

Reb Chaim Sanzer knew his Midrash: "My children are obstinate," God said to Moshe and Aaron, "ill-tempered, troublesome. In assuming leadership over them, expect to be cursed and even stoned by them!"

Those who accept the obligation of Torah leadership become automatic couriers of its sanctity.

Thus, in light of the order "*V'lo sechalelu es sheim kodshi* (You shall not desecrate My holy name)," a transgression known as *chillul Hashem*, pious Torah scholars and leaders must behave in an exemplary manner at all times. If not, they commit a sin even if they have committed *no* sins! (The standard of unbecoming behavior for Torah scholars is strict: it includes being short-tempered, buying something and delaying payment, loud public laughter, not greeting people graciously.)

Rabbi Eliyahu Chaim Meizel of Lodz successfully collected money for various different causes but never got involved in the actual distribution. When asked why, he explained that he preferred to entrust others with the funds so as to avoid ever being accused of mismanagement. He explained that even Moshe, in order to avoid any potential suspicion, was not involved in allocating the funds he collected.

Rav Avraham Shag was so aware of his responsibility in collecting money for others that he always put it into a bag that contained a *mezuza*. This way, if there was a fire on Shabbas, he could carry the money out of the house because it was together with the *mezuza*!

> The *Chofetz Chaim* wanted Rav Avraham Kalmanowitz to open a yeshiva but he was reluctant because it would take too much time away from his own learning.
>
> "If you continue learning for yourself," said the *Chofetz Chaim*, "how

> much will you accomplish in your lifetime? You'll finish *Shas* ten times, or even twenty, but if you open up a yeshiva, you will finish *Shas* over a thousand times through the *talmidim* you produce. This is comparable to a shoe manufacturer. Although he himself doesn't actually make the shoe, his factory will produce more shoes in one week than the shoemaker does in his entire lifetime!"

Similarly, the *Chazon Ish* was quite content to sit and learn his entire life in seclusion. It was only after he heard Rav Chaim Grodzensky and the *Chofetz Chaim*'s opinions that life should be spent helping the *klal* that he moved to Eretz Yisroel and dedicated the rest of his life to building up B'nei Brak.

> When Rav Shlomo Zalman Auerbach became *rosh yeshiva* of *Kol Torah* in Bayit Vegan, he would travel to and from his home in Sha'arei Chesed by bus. The staff of the yeshiva encouraged him to take a taxi at the yeshiva's expense, but he adamantly refused. "The money belongs to the yeshiva and is designated for holy use only, not for taxis!"

Appearances matter, suspicions are deadly.

For this reason a fundraiser cannot go into the offices of the *Beis Hamikdash* (or any *tzedaka* organization) wearing hemmed clothing since money can be hidden in the folds or pockets.

When it comes to giving *tzedaka*, the donor's intentions are irrelevant. The mitzva is available for anyone "whose heart motivates him" to give, even if it's for a personal motive (e.g., giving money to a rebbe in return for a personal bracha).

However, this does not apply to the Jew collecting money. His motives are important to know. Personal objectives disqualify fundraisers: witness the Rambam; he only appointed "God fearing and trustworthy" Jews to run his *tzedaka* fund.

For those in the public eye, the principle of "innocent until proven guilty" does not apply because it's their responsibility not to be under any suspicion!

One day a fundraiser for a Jewish institution came to the home of John McLaughlin.

"We have you down for a $500 pledge," said the fundraiser.

"But that's impossible," said McLaughlin. "I didn't make a pledge. And besides, I'm not even Jewish!"

"I'm sorry," said the fundraiser, "but our institution never makes mistakes. Are you sure you aren't Jewish?"

"How can I prove it to you?" said McLaughlin. "I go to church every Sunday, my father used to direct the Christmas play at school every year, and my mother, *aleiha hashalom*, is buried in a Catholic cemetery."

# Week 30

## On *Loshen Hora*, Slander

With lies you can go far, but not back again!
— *Yiddish folk saying*

Rav Mordechai of Radin was shocked when the *Chofetz Chaim* asked him to arrange a birthday party for him. "I am turning eighty soon," the *tzadik* said, "and I would like to arrange a celebration in honor of this milestone." Rav Sender reminded him that he had spent his life running far from honor!

"Yes," explained the *Chofetz Chaim*, "I have spent my life writing *seforim* on *shmiras haloshen*. But Dovid Hamelech makes it clear that one who is careful not to speak forbidden words will merit a long life, so what would people say if the man who spent his life teaching others to avoid *loshen hora* did not merit longevity? They would assume that I was a hoax. What greater *chilul Hashem* could there be? Therefore, now that *Hashem* has granted me a long life, I wish to express my gratitude and sanctify His name. This would be the sole purpose of my celebration!"

# Watch Your Tongue!

> The Sadigura Rebbe taught his followers that something can be learned from anything.
> "Then tell us, Rebbe," asks a chassid, smiling, "what does a train teach us?"
> "A train can teach us that if a person is sometimes even one second late, he can miss everything!"
> "And Rebbe," asks another, "what can a telegram possibly teach us?"
> "From a telegram we learn that in life every word is counted and we are charged for it!"
> "But Rebbe, what in the slightest can a telephone teach us?"
> "Ahh, from the telephone we learn that everything we say *here* is heard *there*," replied the Rebbe, pointing to the Heavens.

From the wisdom of Sholem Aleichem: If a horse with four legs can sometimes stumble, how much more a man with only one tongue!

In his typically colorful language, Eliezer ben Yitzchak, author of *Orchos Chaim*, advises Jews "not to be like a fly, seeking sore spots; better to cover up your neighbor's flaws than reveal them to the world!"

*Loshen hora*, which literally means "the evil tongue," is unique because its net of iniquity extends further than just the person involved in "excessive chatter." As the Talmud puts it, the gossiper stands in Syria — but kills in Rome! In other words: watch what you say!

The fact that even casual comments can reflect on one's personal integrity is the reason for the order "*Lo yochel d'varo k'chol hayotzei mipiv ya'aseh* (Don't desecrate your word; according to whatever leaves your mouth shall you do)."

Remember: contrary to popular slang, talk is not cheap!

> Rabbi Moshe Midner once discussed a certain matter that pertained to a third person with a *talmid* of the *Chofetz Chaim*. Mention of the person's name caused the *talmid* to twitch his nose in disapproval. Rabbi Moshe Midner immediately cut the conversation short, asking, "Is it permissible to speak *loshen hora* with your nose?"

The *Chofetz Chaim*, whose title comes from a verse in Tehillim ("Who is the man that desireth life…[*chofetz chaim*]…Keep thy tongue from evil!"), listed thirty-one Torah violations from speaking or listening to *loshen hora*. He was convinced that the sin of loose lips was tied in to a lack of *ahavas Yisroel*, "loving other Jews."

If, during a meeting, his visitor would say something negative about another person, the Vizhnitzer Rebbe, Rav Yisroel Hager, would get up and cover the man's mouth so that forbidden speech would not come from it.

And of the forty-three sins listed in the Yom Kippur's *Al Cheit*, no fewer than eleven are tied to speech. So dangerous is the tongue, note Jewish mystics, that God hid it from public view, behind two protective walls (the mouth and teeth) in order to mitigate its misuse.

When ordering "*Lo seileich rachil b'amecha* (A gossipmonger shall not walk among your people)," the Torah dumps "gossipmongers" into the file of evil professions in that they make a career out of searching for tidbits of gossip and then spreading them door-to-door.

Even the words are similar: *rochail* and *rachil*; the first describes "a peddler," the second a gossipmonger who peddles his filthy wares among the people.

> Rav Aaron of Karlin, traveling with a group of wagon drivers, became very uncomfortable when they started speaking *loshen hora*. The *rav* politely interrupted their conversation and for the rest of their journey engaged them in a conversation about the different types and merits of horses. When the group arrived in Mezritch, hundreds of chassidim were waiting to greet Rav Aaron. "Why didn't you tell us you are such a great rabbi?" his surprised fellow travelers asked, "and why were you discussing horses with us the whole way?" Replied Rav Aaron, "I noticed that your words of slander were killing people left, right and center, so I preferred that you direct them at horses instead!"

Rabbi Asher ben Yechiel would fine Jews who shamed others and held special courts to assess damages according to the social status of the offender and victim.

"Have you heard something?" asks ben Sira. If yes, then "let it die with you!"

The only antidote for evil speech, writes Rav Chama bar Chanina, is Torah study, which he infers from the verse "The cure for an evil tongue [*loshen hora*] is [Torah], a tree of life to those who grasp it!"

Moishie is sitting around shmoozing with his friend Yankie.

"You know that Rubinstein guy," Moishie complains. "Well, he's a no-goodnik, dishonest in business, a terrible husband and a lousy father."

"How do you know so much about this Rubinstein guy?" asks Yankie.

"Rubinstein?" Moishie replies. "We've been best friends for years!"

# Week 31

## On *Ma'aser*

Have witnesses when you lend but none when you give.
— *Yiddish folk saying*

A poor chassid came to the home of Rabbi Moshe Chaim Rottenberg, the wealthy brother of the Gerer Rebbe, carrying a letter from the Kotzker Rebbe asking Rav Moshe to provide the man with funds for his daughter's wedding. The *rav* gave him one ruble and wished him well. The chassid left in frustration. After all, it had cost him more than one ruble just to make the trip. While traveling home, he was met by an emissary of Rav Moshe Chaim who handed him the rest of the money he needed to cover his daughter's wedding expenses. The poor chassid was dumbfounded. He immediately turned back and went to Rav Moshe's home.

"What happened?" he asked. "Why did you give me just one ruble initially, and then send an agent with the rest of the donation?"

Rav Moshe Chaim replied, "When you arrived with your letter, I saw that you believed you already had the money in your hands. You had put all your trust in a letter, and forgotten that there is a Creator. Therefore, I put you off momentarily so that you would remember that there is a Creator!"

# The Ten Percent Rule

> The Klausenberger Rebbe often wondered why Jews were so neglectful of the obligation to put aside a tenth of their earnings for *tzedaka*, since it was as much a part of *Shulchan Aruch* as all the other mitzvos they observed. One day a *talmid* asked the Rebbe if he could pay off his debts before giving *ma'aser*. The Rebbe was not at all happy with the question. "If you would come to ask me about the priorities of all of your other expenses," he said, "then I would answer this question as well!"

The *minhag* to "tithe" is derived from Avraham. After returning from a successful battle by the Dead Sea against four kings, the first patriarch gives a tenth of his possessions to Prince Melchizedek of Jerusalem.

The next to tithe is Yaakov. When he flees his father's house to escape Esav's wrath, he makes a vow, "*V'chol asher siten li aser a'asrenu lach* (Whatever [produce] You will give me, I shall repeatedly tithe to you)!" It is from this verse that we get the maximum *ma'aser* to give. From the Torah's use of the compound verb *aser a'asrenu*, "a tenth, a tenth," we learn that Yaakov donated two-tenths (i.e., a fifth).

Why not give more than a fifth? Because over-generous givers take the risk that they themselves may fall on hard times, causing others to have to help them.

> When the Steipler Rav gave money to the poor he would do it behind the closed doors of his study, and then thank the recipient for relieving him of the burden of holding money meant for others. By the time his beneficiaries left the room, they felt that it was they who were doing the Steipler a favor!

The term *tithing* is derived from the Old English *teogoḥa*, which means "tenth"; in Avraham's time it was *esretu*, an Akkadian noun meaning "one-tenth." Originally, based on the command "You will take a tenth of all the produce of your crops," it was thought that tithing applied only to one's crop.

However, it was soon extended to everything on the basis of one extra Torah word, *kol* (all), which teaches that (at least ten percent of) *all* earnings be given to *tzedaka*.

Giving a share to the poor applies to one's income whether it's profit, inheritance, a windfall, interest, or even money or property stolen (or lost) and returned. Why? Because these are considered "new" acquisitions.

So important is distributing money to the poor that Eleazar ben Pedat says that charity grants can even be determined on Shabbas!

A poor woman in Slotzk tried to support herself and her family by selling baked goods. She worked long hours and worked hard but still couldn't make ends meet. Depressed, she went to Rav Isser Zalman Meltzer, *rosh yeshiva* of Eitz Chaim, for advice and a blessing. Rav Isser Zalman advised her to keep a strict account of the money she earned and give a tenth to *tzedaka*. She was shocked. She barely had enough money to feed her children; nevertheless, she did as she was told.

The next week, she brought her tithes, a measly sum, to Rav Isser Zalman to distribute to *tzedaka*. The second week, however, the amount was slightly larger. And so it was, week after week, until the numbers grew to be quite significant. Finally, Rav Isser Zalman told her to stop bringing the money to him and, instead, to distribute the money herself as she saw fit. Years later, her family became one of the wealthiest in Slotzk.

Reb Shneur Zalman was convinced that giving *ma'aser* acted as a magnet with more power to attract God's influence than any other mitzva!

Rav Shach encouraged parents to train their children from a young age to separate a tenth of any money they might receive, and donate it towards the support of Torah study.

Rav Chaim Kanievsky once asked his father, the Steipler, if *ma'aser* money may be used to marry off children. The Steipler chose not to answer this question but replied by simply saying, "One will never become poor from giving *tzedaka* to the poor!"

The rabbi answers the phone and hears, "Hello, is this the rabbi?"

"It is."

"This is the IRS. Can you help us?"

"I can."

"Do you know a Mendy Bauman?"

"I do."

"Is he a member of your congregation?"

"He is."

"Did he donate $10,000 to the synagogue?"

"Not yet, but he will soon!"

# Week 32

## On Making Money, Honesty in Business

You can tell what God thinks of money
by looking at some of the people he gives it to!

— *Yiddish folk saying*

A wealthy individual once went to the *Chofetz Chaim* for advice on how to divide his assets among his children. "I have three sons and one daughter who is married to a well-to-do young man," he said, "and my assets are worth forty thousand rubles."

The *Chofetz Chaim* asked, "And how much do you intend to keep for yourself?"

"No, no. With all due respect, I think you misunderstood. My intention is to divide my assets after my death, not now."

"You don't think you'll need some money for yourself then? With what will you arrive in *Olam Haba*? I suggest leaving a large percent of your assets to *tzedaka*. That way, you can take it with you to the eternal world after your 120 years."

# Even Chanoch Was a Cobbler!

After Rav Yisroel Salanter's rebbetzin purchased a lottery ticket he became very upset, summoned two Jews as witnesses, and declared, "I hereby forfeit all of my rights to my life's belongings, present and future, their fruits and the fruit of their fruits, forever…" Rav Yisroel was afraid of winning the lottery and becoming rich. He was scared of the responsibilities that came with wealth and didn't want to be tested.

"Buy dirt cheap and sell high," the financial advisor told his client. After a few minutes thinking, his client asked, "So, where do I buy dirt?"

Making money is no crime.

Remember: our forefathers were not poor! The Torah reveals that Avraham, Yitzchak and Yaakov were wealthy Jews; and the *brachos* promised by God to Jews in the Holy Land are all materialistic in nature, as are the punishments for violating them.

The *manna* stopped the moment the Jews crossed the Jordan River; from then on, they worked the land as farmers for their livelihood. And every year the *kohen gadol* would emerge from a private room in the Temple on Yom Kippur and beg God to assure that Jews make an honest living and not become charity cases.

Remember: the three main holy places in Israel — the Cave of Machpela, the Temple Mount and Joseph's Tomb — were all purchased with cash, not conquered by the sword.

Jewish law has a lot to say about how to earn and spend money, but never makes economic activity illegitimate. Even Chanoch, reminds the Midrash, the one who "went with God," was a cobbler!

> So scrupulous was Rabbi Chanina in business that one day he mistakenly sold date honey to two customers instead of bee honey, a superior product. Next time the customers came in he apologized but it turned out he was mistaken; they had *wanted* date honey after all!. However, so concerned was he that he nearly derived unfair profit that he donated the sale proceeds to the construction of a new *shul*.

"We are *obligated*," reminds Rebbe Nachman of Breslov, "to engage in commerce and labor."

Interaction among Jews is why a coin was called *lazus* in Hebrew, which means "to move," in that coins (*zuzim*) are intended to "move from one person to another."

The Yiddishists might have been mired in pessimism (As Ibn Ezra said, "If I sold candles, the sun would never set!"), but way before Warren Buffet arrived, the *Midrash Tanchuma* gave solid business advice: "Whatever wares you find lowly and buried in the earth, traffic in them, for they will rise up in the end and you will profit!"

> Once, while walking in the marketplace as a young boy, Rabbi Avraham Bornstein of Sochotshov, the author of *Avnei Nezer*, noticed that someone selling baskets of fruit put good fruits on the top layer of the baskets, whereas beneath them the fruits were rotten. Buyers were deceived to think that all the fruits in the baskets were like those on the top. The boy ran over and overturned all the baskets. Rabbi Avraham's father paid the man for his damages after the vendor complained about the loss of his fruits but refused to rebuke his son for the act, done purely for the sake of Heaven.

Wealth is seen in Jewish tradition as a means of sanctifying life, and helping others less fortunate.

That's why Jews can't charge interest on loans, explains Rav Shimshon Raphael Hirsch, because the money was given by God to be given to others.

Meanwhile Rav Nachman of Kasovir complained to his congregants that "If you think of business when in *shul* is it too much to ask that you think of God when at your business?"

"Not everyone who does much business," concluded Hillel in *Pirkei Avos*, "becomes wise!" Or as one master of *mussar* put it: to be a successful businessman you need extraordinary talents; and if you have such talents, why waste them on business?

The Kapishnitzer Rebbe didn't want his own children to become wealthy because of the difficult spiritual tests associated with money. As the Yiddishists put it: Money is a wonderful thing — but sometimes it's possible to pay too high a price for it!

A little old Jewish lady sold pretzels on a street corner for twenty-five cents each.

Every day a young man would walk by during his lunchtime, and as he passed the pretzel stand, he would leave her a quarter, but never take a pretzel.

And this went on for more then seven years. The two of them never spoke.

One day, as the young man passed the old lady's stand and left his quarter as usual, the pretzel lady finally spoke to him. "Sir, I appreciate your business. You are a good customer, but I have to tell you that the pretzel price has gone up to thirty-five cents!"

# Week 33

## On Making Peace

We should treat enemies like a treasure.
Bury them with care and affection!

— *Yiddish folk saying*

The chassidic rebbe found the secret for peace in the Torah portion of Toldos, and called it his "three times backwards" approach. He explained: "Wherever Avraham went, he looked for water, and dug wells in the Valley of Gerar, but as soon as he had turned his back the local inhabitants filled in the wells. Yitzchak met the same fate. Returning to Gerar, he dug his father's old wells a second time, but once more the local people blocked them up. Yitzchak decided not to fight; if he were to find a home in that region, he would need to live at peace with his neighbors. So the patriarch went on to dig a third well which he called *Rechovot* ("spaciousness"), implying that the land was wide enough for everybody, but once again, for the sake of peace, he had to move on. He finally settled at Beersheva, where at last a peace agreement was entered into with the local people.

It took three episodes of enmity before peace was achieved. How so? Because Yitzchak was prepared to take three steps backwards. This is why Jews do the same at the end of the *Shemoneh Esrei*, whilst saying "*Oseh shalom bimromav, Hu ya'aseh shalom aleinu v'al kol Yisrael* (He Who makes peace in His high places, may He make peace for us and for all Israel!)"

"If you want peace," the rebbe concluded, "you must be willing to step back a little!"

# Pots and Peace

> The Gerer Rebbe once planned to make a "reconciliation visit" to a particular rabbi in the hope that his visit would help build a more positive atmosphere between their chassidim. His followers tried to talk him out of it, saying that it would be a difficult trip and that they would have to walk much of the way on a muddy path. The Rebbe would not hear of canceling his plans. "For the sake of peace, I am willing to walk on the muddy path even ten times!"

The reason the entire House of Israel mourned the death of Aaron and not Moshe, who was only mourned by the men, is because Aaron sought peace amongst families — thus his nickname, *Rodef Shalom*, "one who peruses peace."

Aaron's ability to foster harmony is why Hillel the Elder urged his followers to "be among the disciples of Aaron, loving and pursuing peace, loving people and bringing them closer to Torah."

*Haro'eh kedera bachalom yitzpe l'shalom* is an interesting Torah expression; it means, "If one sees a pot in his dreams he should expect peace."

Pots and peace?

A lesson in the elements explains the connection. Fire and water are total opposites that cannot coexist. Yet they exist if you put a pot, a symbol of *shalom*, between them, thus bringing "peace" between two opposing substances.

Once, after a humiliating experience in trying to make peace between two Jews, the Tchebiner Rav, Rav Dov Berish Weidenfeld, cried, "To imagine peace I dreamt of a pot! And what does the pot get for its efforts? It gets blackened with soot!"

> After Rav Shimshon Raphael Hirsch publicly criticized the ways of the *Haskala* ("Enlightenment," the often fiercely anti-religious embracing of secular knowledge in the eighteenth century), a rabbi wrote to him complaining at his divisiveness. Rav Hirsch responded with a scathing public article, titled "Words of Peace and Truth," wherein he laid out the priorities: "*Shalom* is nothing else but the realization of truth. First truth and only then peace, for peace is not a father of truth; *peace is a child of truth*! When sacred causes are involved [one] must win the people for an inalienable truth that *can never be sold*, not even for the price of peace, and [only] then true, everlasting peace will follow of itself!"

Rav Shimon Shkop of Grodno would intercede even when he saw children fighting over a toy.

Rebbe Nachman of Breslov reconfirmed an old *baraisa* that the only time it was OK to lie was for the sake of domestic peace (*shalom bayis*). Bar Kappara adds: you can even misquote the Torah to bring peace!

But not everything is up for grabs!

Some of the early *maskilim* (adherents of the Haskala) tried to make peace with the nineteenth-century Hungarian Rabbi Moshe Shik (Maharam Shik, the phonetic pronunciation of the acronym for *Moreinu Harav Rabbi Moshe*, "Our Teacher the Rabbi Moshe").

They even quoted the Torah to him: "As you know, our Sages teach that peace is the most important thing of all. Why should there be discord between the *maskilim* and the *yereim* (the God-fearers)?"

In response, the Maharam Shik quoted Zecharia's famous *vort*: "Love truth and peace!" explaining that peace can be built only on truth ("From falsehood we must run far away!").

> "See how all of God's creation borrow from one another," marvels the *Midrash Rabba*. "Day borrows from night, and night from day; the moon borrows from the stars, and the stars from the moon; wisdom borrows from understanding, and understanding from wisdom; the Heavens borrow from the earth, and the earth from the Heavens. All the creations of God borrow from one another, but live in a state of peace without taking one another to court!"

To Eleazar ben Shammua peace was "the essence of all the prophecies"; to Eleazar Hakappar it was "the climax of all blessings"; to the *Zohar* and the Midrash it helped establish the world, was one of God's Names, and formed the basis of an everlasting Covenant with the Jewish people.

If peace is not present, warns the Sassover Rebbe, Moshe Leib, "everything else is lessened!"

Rav Simcha Bunim was more introspective: "It's impossible for you to find peace anywhere…but in your own self!"

At a peace concert in Israel, Bono, U2's lead singer, asks the audience for some quiet. Then he starts to slowly clap his hands. Holding the audience in total silence, he says into the microphone, "I want you to think about something. Every time I clap my hands, a child in Africa dies."

A voice from the front of the audience yells out, "Nu! So stop clapping!"

# Week 34

## On *Midda k'Neged Midda*

You shall tithe so that you will become rich.
— *Yiddish folk saying*

The evening before his wedding, Rav Yosef Chaim Sonnenfeld went to visit his rebbe, the *Ksav Sofer*. His *rebbe* took a pen and paper from his drawer and began to write a certificate of merit for him. Among other things, the *Ksav Sofer* wrote, "There are three qualities which few people have: Torah, fear of God, and good character traits. Chaim possesses them all…"

Out of tremendous modesty, and a fear that reading the letter would have an effect on his *middos*, Rav Yosef Chaim simply folded up the letter without looking at it. He did not open it for twenty years and told no one about it, not even his wife. Only after he turned forty and felt that he could read the letter without its having a negative impact on him did Rav Yosef Chaim allow himself to read what his rebbe had written.

# What Goes 'Round, Comes 'Round!

> After the granddaughter of the Kapishnitzer Rebbe, Rav Avraham Yehushua Heschel, married the son of Rav Shlomo Zalman Auerbach, the Rebbe paid a visit to Rav Shlomo Zalman. At the end of the visit, Rav Shlomo Zalman accompanied the Rebbe out of his house, but the Rebbe's taxi was running late so Rav Shlomo Zalman, who was more than twenty years the Rebbe's junior, asked that a chair be brought for Rav Avraham Yehoshua Heschel while they waited. The Rebbe however, refused to sit, explaining, "My father taught me that before one does any actions, he should think that his action is being photographed. How will it look in Heaven when they see me sitting and Rav Shlomo Zalman standing?"

The principle of *midda k'neged midda*, "*a measure for a measure*," is applicable in both good and bad contexts.

Because Yosef took responsibility for burying his father, his burial was handled by Moshe himself; and because of Moshe's *chesed*, his own burial was handled by none other than God Himself.

And in reverse, to dispel the idea of a having "stroke of bad luck," the response to tragedy, notes Meiri, is not "what did they do?" but "what did I do to deserve this punishment?"

Hopefully, the punishment fits the crime, within the human understanding of both punishment and crime. Take, for example, the repulsive infliction of *tzara'as*, which requires isolation.

Rashi sees a cause-and-effect link of *tzara'as* to evil speech, an act that "separates" husbands from wives, friends from each other.

Other examples abound: Shimshon "eyed" a woman from Timna and had his own eyes gouged out by the Philistines; Avshalom had enormous pride in his hair, so he was ultimately hung by his hair; Lot's wife is turned into a pillar of salt after, says the Midrash, she asked a neighbor if she could borrow salt, implying she had guests (a request that put their lives in danger since guests were *verboten* in Sodom).

> One Chanuka, Rav Yisroel Salanter had to travel to a nearby city for an important meeting. Before he left, he asked his wife to prepare Chanuka candles for him to take along. Surprised, she said to her husband, "But you'll be back in just a few hours!" Rav Yisroel explained that he wanted to be prepared in case a problem arose on the way. Sure enough, his carriage broke down, causing a long delay. When Rav Yisroel finally reached his destination, he paid the wagon driver more than the set price because he

was concerned that it was his own pessimistic comments that had brought about the trouble with the wagon!

So do we really see the consequences of our actions so immediately? And if so, can the principle of *midda k'neged midda* even affect our lifespan?

The verse "The number of your days shall I fill" was proof to Rabbi Akiva that a person doesn't live more than the number of years predestined prior to birth, regardless of his deeds.

One could subtract from that time for bad deeds and sins, but Rabbi Akiva didn't believe that one got "credits" (i.e., additional years) for Torah and mitzvos, which are rewarded in other ways.

But the rabbis of the Talmud disagreed: a person could *both* lose *or* add to his longevity, they argued, based on his actions.

The Gemora recounts how the Angel of Death once took a woman's life before her time due to mistaken identity. Not wanting to return her, he simply added her unfinished years to a Torah scholar worthy of more life. Rabbi Akiva said this proved nothing: between them, they still lived the same number of predestined allocated years!

> Rav Yehuda Hachassid tells the story of a Jew who used to share in the suffering of mourners by taking off his own shoes to show that he shared their pain. On the day that he died, it was Tisha b'Av, and therefore all the Jews in the city walked without shoes. Rav Yehuda was convinced that Hashem had arranged for the man to pass away on Tisha b'Av to show that his conduct was favorable in His eyes.

Several mitzvos that carry a cause-and-effect reward of longevity include honoring of parents, shooing away a mother bird from its nest before taking its eggs (*shiluach hakein*) and charity.

The *Zohar* adds several more, including "collectors of charity" who receive a reward "equivalent to the reward of all those who donate"!

And then there is proportion.

"Small sins are great," reminds Avraham ibn Ezra, "when great people commit them!"

Jewish mystics even tie the extent of reward to the *quality* of a mitzva: "The reward you receive for your charity is entirely dependent on the kindness in your giving!"

"My grandfather always said, 'Don't watch your money; watch your health.' So one day while I was watching my health, someone stole my money. It was my grandfather." — Jackie Mason

# Week 35

## On Modesty, Humility, Pride

> If you cannot be an Elijah,
> then at least be content to be an Elisha!
>
> — *Yiddish folk saying*

There was a very pious charitable Jew whose donations became smaller as he grew wealthier. Once, during a visit, his rebbe put his arm around him whilst they were standing at the window, and the rebbe asked him, "What do you see?"

"I see people in the streets, men and women, young and old."

The rebbe then gave him a mirror and said, "Now tell me what you see."

"What do you mean? I see myself."

"That's right," the rebbe explained. "Both the mirror and the window are made of glass. The only difference between them is that the window is clear and the mirror is backed by silver. Before you had silver, you were able to see other people's needs and others' problems. Since the glass became coated, you are only able to see yourself!"

# What Came First? The Gnat or Man?

> Rabbi Chaim Brisker needed to discuss something with the Rabbi of Narodno so he hired a carriage and went to his home. When he arrived, the *rav* was perplexed. "If the Brisker Rav needed me, I would have gladly come to your house. Why did you trouble yourself to come all the way here? And if you did it out of humility, then, tell me please, do you think it is fair to make me haughty so that you can practice your modesty?!"

Want modesty? Remember: the gnat was created *before* man!

The most humble of them all, defined by God Himself, was Moshe, an *anav mikol adam*, with "*adam*" becoming the acronym for the three greatest paragons of Torah humility: Avraham ("I am but dust and ash"), King David ("But I am a worm, not a man") and the brothers Moshe and Aaron ("What are we?").

In order to stress the importance of humility, the Mishna uses a double adjective in its instruction: "Be exceedingly (*me'od me'od*) humble in spirit."

> While traveling to collect funds for his yeshiva, Rav Elchonon Wasserman always gravitated towards the back of a *shul*. The rabbis of these *shuls*, however, felt uncomfortable that such an important *rav* sat in the back while they sat up front. "Isn't your behavior artificial modesty?" they asked. But Rav Elchonon had already discussed this with the *Chofetz Chaim*, who told him, "It's still better than sitting at the front of the *shul* and thinking in your heart that you are not worthy of such respect!"

To be "very, very" humble is why the *Chofetz Chaim* strived to practice modesty to the extreme.

In a supreme display of discipline, he always dressed in simple clothing, simple boots, and wore a simple cap (which he changed on Shabbas for a simple velvet cap). He ate simple foods with simple utensils on simple functional chairs arranged around simple unpainted tables.

Annoyed when addressed with exaggerated titles and excessive praise, the *Chofetz Chaim* pleaded with other rabbis to stop referring to him as "*Harav Haga'on*." He begged bookstores not to focus on him but on his *seforim*. And as more and more halachic questions came in for him from abroad, he placed ads in newspapers saying, "*Baruch Hashem* the generation is not an 'orphaned' one as there are many qualified local rabbis who should be consulted. There is no reason for people abroad to send their queries to me!"

When Reb Meir Sholom of Porisov arrived in Garbolin the local chassidim greeted him with a grand ceremony. Reb Meir told them that either way there was no need for them to grant him honor. "If I enjoy the honor you grant me, then I obviously don't deserve it. So you might say, 'We know the rebbe doesn't take pleasure in honor. On the contrary, it disturbs him greatly.' In that case, I ask you, 'Why would you want to cause me pain?'"

The *Orchos Tzadikim* was convinced that the ladder leading to God was made out of humility, the rungs out of everything else. One small modest mitzva gets you further up the ladder of humility!

It is written in Eliyahu Hacohen's *Shevet Mussar*, chapter 17: "He who humbles himself, God uplifts; and he who raises himself, God lowers. He who pursues fame and honor, honor runs from him; and he who runs from honor, fame and honor chase after him!"

The question is obvious: why repeat this lesson twice?

The second time around is a subtle message: don't even think of lowering yourself with the expectation that God will uplift you in return!

Nearing death, the Ba'al Shem Tov hinted to his disciples that they should start looking for a new rabbi of the city.

"But how will we know who is the one?"

"Ask him for a way to avoid haughtiness," answered the Ba'al Shem Tov. "If he suggests a specific technique, know that he is not worthy of being the city's *rav*. However, if he says that there is no way and that only Hashem can help if you ask Him fervently enough, then he is the one to whom you should cling!"

Good deeds without humility? The *Sefer Chassidim* says they are akin to a dish without water! And the Talmud adds: be humble, that you may not be humbled!

What if we had no Torah? In that case, posits Yochanan ben Nappacha, we would learn modesty from cats, honest toil from ants, chastity from doves.

When Rav Yehuda Hachassid was asked the reason for his longevity, he quoted King Solomon: "God gives favor to the humble!"

The tough school principal is walking down the corridor and bumps into a student. He pats the little boy on the head, and says, "Hi. What's your name?"

"Baruch," the boy answers.

"And how old are you, Baruch?"

"Eight."

"Shame on you!" the principal replies. "By your age, I was nine already!"

# Week 36

## On Patience, Persistence

Drive your horse not with a whip but with oats!
— *Yiddish folk saying*

Rav Avraham Mordechai Alter was a remarkably patient man. On one of his visits to Vienna, the Rebbe was honored to be the *sandek* at a *bris*. Being his punctual self, the Rebbe arrived exactly on time. However, the *ba'al simcha* was waiting for another Rebbe to arrive to begin the ceremony, and this Rebbe arrived almost two hours late. A guest at the *bris* later shared his observations: "I stood beside the Gerer Rebbe as he waited, wrapped in his *tallis*, for close to two hours without even asking the reason for the delay. It was impossible to discern even the slightest expression of annoyance on his face. He simply waited patiently without saying a word."

# Sounds of Silence

> When people spoke negatively about Rav Simcha Zissel, the Alter of Kelm, Rav Simcha would express pleasure that his faults were finally being revealed to the public. Once, a *cheder* rebbe attacked the Alter with dreadful accusations, calling him a *rasha* who would have no place in *Olam Haba*. Yet the Alter leaned even closer to hear more clearly. When someone tried to silence the offender, the Alter stopped him, saying his accuser was right and was only revealing the truth!

Moshe ibn Ezra was convinced: the one who persists in knocking is the one who will succeed in entering! The Talmud praises patience, especially when shown by those who are shamed publicly and hold their tongues.

This ability not to respond negatively is considered such a virtue that the disciplined silence is rewarded on Rosh Hashana ("He will be cleansed of his sins!").

"One can achieve far more through patience than he can through anger!" taught Rav Chaim Volozhiner, who was legendarily patient.

"I have found nothing better," writes the perceptive sage Rabban Shimon ben Gamliel, "for oneself than silence!"

> This is how Rav Chaim Sanzer discovered the virtues of patience: "When I was young I wished I could correct the entire world to the service of *HaKadosh Boruch Hu*. Later on in life I realized that this was impossible, so I tried to set the people of my own city straight. Then I said, 'If only I could influence the members of my family…' Finally, I realized I was aiming too high and resolved to work on *my own* observance of the mitzvos!" In humility, Rav Chaim added, "Regrettably, I have been unsuccessful even in this!"

After staring at Mother Nature, Job finally gets it: water wears down stone!

The *Chofetz Chaim* eloquently described the benefits of patience for parents: "If the father, the locomotive of his family, is strong enough to climb the difficult hill while controlling his actions, then all his children will follow suit. However, if he loses control, all the cars will tumble down the mountain with him — and will be crushed!"

Rav Reuven Grozovsky never punished his children when he saw them do something wrong. He waited until the time was right, knowing that patience was a necessary ingredient in raising children.

After the Mishna lists three things a Jew must say just before *Shabbas* ("Have you tithed? Have you prepared the *eruv*? Have you lit *Shabbas* candles?"), Rabba bar Rav Huna adds a reminder: if you want to be heard, ask them softly!

> After the *Chazon Ish* once harshly criticized a particular rabbi for his conduct, Rabbi Eliezer Plachinsky tried to excuse the rabbi: "This incident was an exception; he lost sight of reason because of a personal bias…" 'That's exactly the point!" the *Chazon Ish* exclaimed. "If you were to tell me that the *gadol hador* had a mishap and transgressed a grave sin, I would accept your argument. But a personal bias? Everyone has his preferences twenty-four hours a day, and if one allows these feelings to get in his way, how will he ever become a *gadol*?"

The *Chazon Ish* had legendary patience. He was known to have said, "I can listen to someone tell me the same story three times without interrupting him even once!"

When asked how he could listen to so much *narishkeit* (foolishness), he replied, "I am like the miller who spends every working hour with the rumble of the mill behind him. The miller is so accustomed to the noise that if the wheels were to stop, he would probably get a headache from the quiet!"

> One evening, the Gerer Rebbe's chassidim crowded into the *beis medrash* to watch the Rebbe light Chanuka candles, but just as the Rebbe was about to recite the *bracha*, someone bumped into the menorah and it fell to the ground. Everyone froze in shock. The Rebbe, on the other hand, remained calm as usual. With complete peace of mind, he simply picked up the menorah, refilled its oil cups, and began the *brachos* as though everything had gone exactly as planned.

Wanting to instill discipline and patience (*sitzfleisch*) in their students, the directors of one of the great yeshivas in Europe instituted a five-minute study period. Each *bochur* was obligated to pick a *sefer* at the same time every day, sit down quietly, and learn for five minutes until he finished it, a period of several months.

Aside from the content, the *bochurim* learned the lesson of patience and persistence, flip sides to the same coin! The righteous man, reminds *Mishlei*, falls down seven times — yet rises up again!

A guy was pushing a stroller with a screaming baby in the supermarket saying to himself, repeatedly, "Moishie, don't get excited; Moishie, don't yell; Moishie, keep calm."

A passerby approached him, saying, "You certainly are to be commended for your patience and for trying to soothe your son Moishie."

He looked at her and said, "Lady, I'm Moishie!"

# Week 37

## On Prayer

When I was young I used to pray for a bicycle.
Then I realized that God doesn't work that way.
So I stole a bicycle and prayed for forgiveness.

— *Yiddish folk saying*

A Karliner Chassid was in Vienna over Shabbas and decided to *daven* in the *beis medrash* of the Chortkover Rebbe. Before Shabbas he asked the Rebbe if he could, according to Karliner *minhag*, *daven* loudly. "Absolutely not!" replied the Rebbe. "You must *daven* quietly and with awe. This is our *minhag* and I expected you to follow it."

So on Shabbas the Karliner Chassid made a tremendous effort to *daven* silently. However, when he came to *Nishmas Kol Chai* he could no longer contain himself and shouted out the entire chapter at the top of his lungs.

After *davening*, he felt terrible and went over to the Rebbe to apologize.

"No need," shrugged the Rebbe, "Better a heartfelt scream than a silent, cold prayer."

"But the Rebbe strongly forbade me…"

Smiling, the Chortkover Rebbe explained, "If I'm told in advance about the shouting, I have to object; however, if, in the midst of *davening*, one becomes so overwhelmed that he cannot contain his cries, how can I object to this superior *tefilla!*"

# From Your Mouth to God's Ear!

> When criticized for moving during *davening*, the Ba'al Shem Tov replied, "Perhaps we move in this manner to wave off unwelcome thoughts that would interrupt our prayer. Would it be unusual to see that a person drowning goes through strange motions doing whatever was necessary to save his life?"

Jewish prayer is called *tefilla*, from the root *palal*, "to judge, to intercede."

The Rambam adds the component of *kavana*, "concentration, direction, inwardness."

Bachya ibn Pakuda clarifies, "Prayer without *kavana* is like a body without a soul or a husk without a kernel."

The Steipler Rav called the Manchester Gaon, Rav Yehuda Zev Segal, "the pillar of *tefilla*" after seeing the pages of his siddur moist from tears.

Rabbi Moshe ben Yosef di Trani (*Maharit*), a big proponent of the idea that "God only helps those who help themselves," defined prayer as "the act in which man asks God for something he needs which he cannot acquire by his own efforts."

Meanwhile, a word of advice from Rabbi Meir: "When speaking to God, keep your words few!"

> When my son was only seven years old, he asked to come along with me to *shul* one Shabbas morning. I said no and he stayed home. Several minutes later I felt sorry I had left him at home so I went back to get him. As I was walking up the path, Shimshon, fully dressed for *shul*, was already running towards me. "Where are you going?" I asked.
>
> "Tatte," he replied, 'I begged Hashem that you would change your mind and I was so sure that He would listen to my *tefilla* that I started making my way...!"

Avraham established an important principle: pray *before*, not after, adversity arrives. Why? Because the Torah prefers preemptive precautionary prayer ("medication *before* the infection"), since preventing a catastrophe is easier than relieving one.

The welfare of other Jews, reminds Rav Yehuda Hachassid, is already a basic responsibility of each Jew ("When *they* become ill, *my* clothing is sackcloth!"), but extending one's concern for the enemy, a stunning ability to rise above normal impulses, increases the chances that one's own prayer will be heard!

The lesson is this: if prayers for an enemy's welfare are expected, how then can we not pray on behalf of those who cause us no harm? The Vilna Gaon thus defines the most ideal kind of prayer as the one that seeks to help another Jew.

Rav Chaim Yitzchok Korb, the soft-spoken *rosh yeshiva* in Chicago, never asked a student if he had *davened* — which he thought was God's concern, not his — but he made a point of inquiring whether the boy had eaten properly.

The Koretzer Rebbe, Pinchas Shapiro, on prayer: "It is the nature of gold and silver that they are refined through the heat of fire. If we, after we have prayed, do not feel that we have been refined and improved, then maybe the reason is that we are made of a baser metal or our prayer was not filled with enough fire!"

> Rav Avraham Yafen once approached the *Chofetz Chaim* and asked him for a blessing that he would have children. "I bless you and I will pray for you," replied the *Chofetz Chaim*. "However, you should know that God wants you to pray. It is difficult for anyone to experience the degree of your own pain, so your own *tefillos* are the most beneficial."

The Yiddishists had a priority of prayer: if a Jew breaks a leg, he thanks God he didn't break both legs; if he breaks both, he thanks God he did not break his neck!

What happens to all our prayers? An angel collects them all, explains the Midrash, weaves them into garlands, and places them on God's Head.

Rabbi Simcha Zissel Broide, the *Alter* of Kelm, said the most potent of all prayers are those of the totally helpless. Prayer, concludes Reb Eleazar, can be more effective than good deeds, noting that God allowed Moshe to view Eretz Yisroel not because of his good deeds — but on account of his prayers!

The final word goes to Rebbe Nachman of Breslov: Don't pray when you're angry; God's not listening!

Moishie's walking down a street in Brooklyn when he hears noises coming from an old deserted warehouse. He goes over and peeks through the window and sees a huge altar up front with a big ZERO painted on it. The room is full of white-robed folks with the word "NIL" painted on their robes, chanting hymns to the altar and singing prayers and praise to "The Blessed Nothingness."

As a woman steps out of the building, Moishie turns to her and says, "What's going on in there? Is nothing sacred to you?!"

# Week 38

## On Rebuke, Offering Advice

Better to be good than to be pious!
— *Yiddish folk saying*

> The *Chazon Ish* was convinced that his ability to inspire and influence others was due to his silence. He seldom spoke his mind to others or chastised them for wrongdoing. Once, when asked to speak out on a specific issue, he responded, "Don't you understand? People listen to me specifically because I am particular not to speak sharply!"

"Just as it is a mitzva to speak words that will be heard," replied the *Chazon Ish* when asked about actively protesting Shabbas desecration, "so is it a mitzva to remain silent in the presence of those who will not listen!" Why? Far better to do an *aveira* obliviously than consciously. And more! No Jew is allowed to instill hatred in another ("Do not rebuke a scoffer lest he hate you!").

# The *Tzadik* in Peltz

> One Shabbas an irreligious man knocked on Rav Yehuda Tzadka's door and introduced himself to the *rosh yeshiva*. "I am a taxi driver who drives on Shabbas. One Shabbas I drove by you in the street and you bitterly cried out "*Shabbas! Shabbas!*" to me. It was not the same as the other shouts. I could hear that it was sincere and pure, and it has continued to bother me so much that I decided to find out who you were. Now that I've found you, perhaps you can tell me why it hurts you so much!"

Rav Yehuda was not a serial rebuker; in fact he only shouted "*Shabbas*" if he thought it would have an effect. How did he know who to shout at? Only at those who were driving slowly, on the assumption that those speeding no longer cared.

> The Satmar Rav once asked Rav Amram Blau to continue his protests of *chilul Shabbas* and *treif* food in Jerusalem. Rav Amram complained that he was the only one present at these protests. "Why don't other religious Jews go out to defend the Torah?"
>
> "Just be glad," replied the Satmar Rav, "that they don't protest your protests!"

If done properly, *tochacha*, which literally means "correction" (as in correcting another for doing something wrong) is a mitzva; but, warns Rabbi Chaim of Velozhin, unless it's done with *seichel*, in a "pleasant-toned voice," the mitzva to admonish does not apply.

Reb Chaim had a unique ability to revive the spirits of Jews in distress just through kind words; in response, Jews with *tzores* would literally rejoice in his presence.

"My father would perpetually remind me," Reb Chaim's son recalled, "that man wasn't created for himself but to help others!"

In fact, it's forbidden to embarrass another Jew, child or adult, in public — or even in private! ("One who shames a Jew in public has no portion in the World to Come!") Yet to offer the right words of encouragement to the right person at the right time is an art ("Beware," Rabbi Akiva warns, "of unsolicited advice!").

> Rav Eliyahu Dessler, *mussar* master, once wrote a letter of rebuke to a student: "I did not find in your letter, which you sent me, even one word of gratitude. I want you to understand that I am not chastising you because I was hurt in any way. I am telling you off because I love you. I simply do not want you to be an ingrate!"

Rav Shmuel Wosner once commented: "If I raise my voice in rebuke, I will lose any chance of being listened to. Then I will have lost more than I gained!"

Remember: it's a myth that comforting others is limited to just periods of mourning.

There's an overall obligation to offer support in all moral, financial and social circumstances. Every person, according to Mordechai Yosef of Ishbitz, reaches God through his *chesronos* (deficiencies). However, before jumping to conclusions, Hillel gives the commonsense warning, "Do not judge someone else until you have been in his position!" Thus, argues Rav Chaim Soloveitchik, the status quo of every Jew is that "he is good!" In halachic terms, he is a *chezkas kashrus*, akin to "an immovable wall"!

Rav Avraham Pam would often point to Bilam's donkey (whose perception of spiritual reality was apparently greater than his master's) as compelling proof that not everything is what it seems to be, that what the eye sees is often superficial.

Reish Lakish, a Talmudic-era sage, once led a band of criminals but returned to Torah after an encounter with Rabbi Yochanan. Shneur Zalman of Liadi, founder of Chabad, credits Lakish's return to Rabbi Yochanan's ability to redirect his altruistic energy away from vice to merit.

> When asked how can Orthodox Jews *daven* three times a day, go to *shiurim*, give *tzedaka*, send their children to yeshiva, eat only kosher, and still cheat in business, Rav Yaakov Kamenetsky replied, "That's the wrong question. The real question is, 'How can immoral and unethical people *daven* three times a day, go to *shiurim*, give *tzedaka*, send their children to yeshiva, and eat only kosher?"

The Yiddishists would have a saying: the *tzadik in peltz*, which means "the pious person with the fur coat" — an allusion to the person who says, "I'm warm. I have a coat. If you are cold, it's not my problem!"

When asked, "Is it permitted in Jewish law to throw stones at other Jews on Shabbas?" the wise Rebbe replied, "Is it permitted to throw stones at other Jews *even* on a weekday?"

A United States Marine was attending some college courses between assignments in Iraq and Afghanistan. One day a professor who was an avowed atheist walked into the class, looked at the ceiling and threw out a challenge: "God, if you are real, then I want you to knock me off this platform. I'll give you exactly fifteen minutes."

The class was shocked. You could hear a pin drop. After ten minutes the professor said, "Well, God, I'm still waiting." At the last minute the Marine got out of his chair, walked up to the professor, and knocked him across the face, making him fall off the stage. He then returned to his seat.

"What's the matter with you?!" the shaken professor screamed. "What was that for?"

"Well," the Marine calmly replied, "God's too busy protecting our soldiers who are protecting your right to say stupid stuff — so, He sent me!"

# Week 39

## On Respecting Elders, Honoring *Talmidei Chachamim*

You can't help someone uphill without
getting closer to the top yourself!

— *Yiddish folk saying*

The two esteemed Torah giants Rabbi Akiva Eiger, the Rav of Poznan, and Rabbi Yaakov, the Rav of Lissa, happened to be one Shabbas in the same town. Rav Eiger was known for his incredible humility in spite of being one of the most outstanding sages of his generation. When he was called up to the reading of the Torah for *shlishi* (the more honorable aliya), he all but fainted. The people present were alarmed without knowing the cause for his faintness but Rav Yaakov realized that Rav Eiger was shocked by the lack of Torah respect for not having bestowed upon Rav Yaakov the honor of *shlishi*.

Rav Yaakov knew that the only way to restore his well-being was to appease his mind and approached Rabbi Eiger whispering, "Your honor should realize that Poznan is a bigger city than Lissa and as such the *shlishi* is awarded in honor of the larger populace." Hearing this, Rabbi Akiva Eiger's strength slowly returned and he was able to approach the *sefer Torah*.

# The "Wings of Israel"

When Rav Yehuda Tzadka and Rav Bentzion Abba Shaul were to speak at Yeshiva Porat Yosef, each was adamant that the other speak first. Rav Tzadka prevailed and Rav Abba Shaul got up to speak.

"Do you know why I'm speaking first?" he told his audience. "For the same reason that one is not permitted to eat anything after the *afikoman* because the Torah wants the taste of the mitzva to remain with us for as long as possible. Therefore, I, too, want you to retain the flavor of the *rosh yeshiva*'s wonderful words."

When Rav Tzadka began his speech, he said, "In truth, I should not speak at all in order not to spoil the flavor of Rav Bentzion's precious remarks…but what I can I do? My friends have pressured me to say a few words!"

This exchange allowed a room full of *yeshiva bochurim* to witness the grace and honor between Torah teachers, a fulfillment of a Gemora, "See how they love and respect each other!"

"I would often make a conscious decision to speak to the *Chofetz Chaim*," Rav Elchonon Wasserman recalls, "however, each time I came into his presence, I felt as if I was standing in front of an angel. I was completely overwhelmed, and lost my power of speech!"

Whenever the Judean king Yehoshafat saw a *talmid chacham* he always displayed *emunas chachamim* (faith in Torah scholars) by rising from his throne, hugging and kissing him, proclaiming, "*Rebbe, Rebbe*, my master, my master!"

Rav Chaim Soloveitchik, *av beis din* of Brisk, used to rise when his son, and later his successor, Reb Velvele, entered the room. The father was convinced his son was a great *talmid chacham*, but his son was embarrassed at his father's act. So he used to climb through the window to enter his father's house in order to avoid walking past him by going through the front door and troubling him to rise.

A table, says the Midrash, is not blessed if it has not fed Torah scholars!

And to dine with a Torah scholar, adds the Talmud, is to feast also with the *Shechina*; another Midrash compares respect for scholars to the pegs and chords that hold up a tent — in this case, the people of Israel.

> Rabbi Mordechai Elefant recalls: "I once saw Rav Yitzchak Ze'ev Soloveitchik of Brisk engaged in a discussion with Rav Shach, who was leaning forward with his knees bent in a very odd position. Rav Shach later explained, 'The Brisker Rav asked me to sit down, but obviously didn't realize there was no chair. I didn't want to correct him so I leaned forward to make it seem as though I was sitting!'"

Rabbi Yehoshua ben Levi taught his sons to show respect even to a senile scholar even though he had forgotten all his Torah learning, explaining that even the broken Ten Commandments were placed in the Ark together with the whole one.

When Rav Yisroel Gustman, long-serving *dayan* of Rav Chaim Ozer Grodzensky's Vilna *beis din*, dropped in to visit the Tchebiner Rav in Jerusalem, the Rebbe quickly ran to don his hat and recite the special *bracha* of seeing a unique *talmid chacham*.

The Maharil Diskin was once in the home of a famous financier when a poor yeshiva student entered the room. While rising from his seat to greet the young man, the Maharil noticed that his host did not budge. "Stand up!" cried the Maharil. "A yeshiva student is standing before you!" The Maharil made it clear that the young man was to be honored because he studied Torah.

> One Shabbas afternoon Rav Berel Kruezer, a guest in a *shul*, was listening to a *d'var Torah*, unaware that everybody had already *davened mincha*. When it became obvious the speaker would end after Shabbas, Rav Berel quietly stepped back to *daven* out in the corridor. The next morning he asked the *Chazon Ish* if he had done the right thing. "This is an issue of *halbonas panim*," replied the *Chazon Ish*. "Leaving in the middle of a speech is not only disrespectful to the speaker, it is positively humiliating to him. There is no excuse to treat a *talmid chacham* this way, and you should not have left the room to *daven*!"

"How silly people are," sighs Rava. "They rise before a Torah scroll but not before a Torah scholar!"

Rabbi Akiva compared the children of Israel to birds, and their wings, without which they couldn't fly, to *zekeinim*, "elderly Jewish sages."

A grandson calls to wish his grandmother Happy Birthday, and asks her, "How old are you, Bubbe?"

"I'm sixty-two," she replies.

He pauses for a minute, and asks, "Did you start at one?"

# Week 40

## On Selfishness, Sensitivity

> If you rub shoulders with a rich man,
> you may just get a hole in the sleeve!
> — *Yiddish folk saying*

Someone asked a *bochur* to step aside at a funeral procession to let Rabbi Yisroel Yaakov Kanievsky pass. The Steipler Rav noticed and said, "Why do you bother him? Am I more important than he is?"

When the Steipler would give *shiurim* in Yeshivas Beis Yosef, students from the Slabodka Yeshiva would come to listen, causing the unassuming Steipler to comment, "I don't understand why people come to listen to my *shiur*; it is *bitul Torah* on their part!"

On the *yahrzeit* of the *Chazon Ish*, the Steipler's *d'var Torah* in his honor attracted an overflowing crowd. The Steipler began by relating how the *Chofetz Chaim* had once been in Bialystok and hundreds had crammed into the room to see him.

Surprised, the *Chofetz Chaim* turned to someone and asked, "What is it, am I a hunchback?"

# Sensitive to Sensitivity

> During World War I, Rav Boruch Ber Leibowitz, *rosh yeshiva* of Kaminetz, was traveling by train with his family to Poland. At one station, filled with soldiers, an elderly Jewish woman and her daughter were denied access to the train. Seeing this, Rav Boruch Ber decided not to continue, explaining, "I'm not going to leave an elderly woman and her daughter here alone among soldiers!" So, his entire family got off the train and kept them company until they could all board the next train, together!

The ability to feel, and then share, the needs and troubles of others (being *nosei b'ol chaveiro*) is a rare and remarkable quality. Very few have it.

This requires shedding your selfishness, and breaking out from your own little world into the complexity of others where their joy is not only your joy, their laughter is not only your laughter — but their pain is also your pain!

Suddenly, you are in reach of the Mother of all Mitzvos: loving your fellow as yourself!

> After obtaining an approbation from Rav Eliyahu Chaim Meisels, the Lodzer Rav, for his *Sefer Achiezer*, Rav Chaim Ozer Grodzensky asked the Lodzer Rav, "Why haven't you published your own *chiddushim* for others to see? They are brilliant!"
>
> "Oh, I do have *chiddushim* in a book," the Rav proudly replied, "let me show you." Rav Elya then brought out a ledger and gave it to Rav Chaim, who anxiously opened the first page and was surprised to see a long list of names.
>
> "Yes, these are my *chiddushim* that will accompany me to *Olam Haba*. They are lists of widows and orphans that I support, the poor people I send money to, and the different organizations of *chesed* that I raise money for!"

The structure of the *siddur* is a daily reminder. All pleas to God are in plural: "Heal *us*," "See *our* suffering," etc. This is a clue, explains Rav Yehuda Hachassid, why some prayers are answered quicker than others; the Jew who feels no need to pray for a friend is less deserving of having his own prayer answered.

Rav Moshe Feinstein was one of the first to purchase a certain beautiful Shas after World War II, the first of its kind in the United States. One day a *talmid* accidentally spilled a bottle of ink onto the *Gemora*. He felt terrible and was in fear of the reaction. But when Rav Moshe returned to his office, he simply smiled and said, "Blue is my favorite color" — and continued his learning!

> Rav Isser Zalman Meltzer was so sensitive about honoring every individual that when he wasn't sure he was ready to give the proper respect, he would excuse himself from his study for a few minutes, go into the next room, pace back and forth, mumbling several times to himself, "Let your friend's honor be dearer to you than your own...," until he felt he was ready to greet the visitor properly. He would then return to his desk and restart the conversation!

Rav Yisroel Zev Gustman was extra-sensitive to the feelings of others. The *rosh yeshiva* never accepted the honor of being a *sandek* at a *bris mila* unless he was sure that both grandfathers had already been given this honor. To students who asked him to be *sandek*, he would say, "I will, *im yirtze Hashem*, be *sandek* at your third son's bris!"

The Vizhnitzer Rebbe, Rabbi Yisroel Hager, treated everyone with great respect, always tipping his hat to non-Jews he passed on the street. Rav Itzel Peterburger, despite his elderly age, would bend down and sweep out under his bed every morning, explaining, "Why should the maid have the difficult job of cleaning up the mess I made?"

> Rabbi Nosson Adler, the *Chasam Sofer*'s mentor, once traveled a long way in freezing weather to be *sandek* at a *bris*. But when the *seuda* began the family noticed that Rav Nosson was missing. Worried, they searched everywhere until they found him standing outdoors, shivering in the cold, watching the horse and buggy that had brought him.
>
> "Why are you outside?" asked the *ba'al simcha*. Rav Nosson explained that it wasn't fair to leave the wagon driver outside, alone in the cold, while everybody else was warm indoors, "So I offered to switch places for awhile so that he could warm up as well."

And the Torah's sensitivity to being sensitive even crept into Jewish law on the side of the guilty.

The fine for stealing an ox is five oxen, explains Rashi, but only four if you steal a sheep. Why? Because the thief has already suffered embarrassment by having to carry it home on his shoulders!

Little Sammy gets separated from his *zeidy* at the circus, so he goes up to a policeman and says, "I've lost my grandfather!"

The cop asks, "What's he like?"

Little Sammy replies, "Beer and sports!"

# Week 41

## On *Shalom Bayis*

Love is the best relationship, wisdom the best ancestor.
— *Yiddish folk saying*

A young couple on the verge of breaking up went to see Rav Shimshon Pincus. The *rav* descided to speak to them separately. He first asked the wife what was going on.

"I can't take it anymore," she exclaimed. "We've been married over a year and my husband never, ever smiles."

Rav Shimshon then went to the other room and asked her husband, "How come you never smile?"

Quite embarrassed, he explained that he had very crooked teeth and that this made his smile very ugly. Being embarrassed, he tried not to smile.

"Why don't you get your teeth fixed?"

"I would love to have nice teeth, but there is no way I can afford the orthodontic work."

Rav Shimshon then quickly raised the money and gave it to the husband, ordering him, "For the sake of *shalom bayis*, get your teeth straightened right away!"

# For Domestic Bliss Do All the Don'ts!

> A tale from the Gemora: One *erev Shabbas*, Reb Meir was passing by a house and heard a couple arguing and fighting. For the next three consecutive *arvei Shabbas*, Reb Meir made a point of dropping in to that family for a visit. The couple obviously were not going to fight in front of a major Torah sage so the house remained peaceful. After Reb Meir left from his third weekly visit, the Satan also left the house, complaining, "Woe is me for I have been chased out of that home!' Then *shalom bayis* was restored to that household.

When asked for advice on raising good children, Rav Pam would often quote the Steipler Rav's two-ingredient recipe: fifty percent *tefilla* and fifty percent *shalom bayis*!

As it relates to *shleimus*, "completeness," *shalom*, as in the absence of tension in the home, is insufficient. The Torah wants *shalom* with a "wholeness" that only comes from the presence of harmony, cooperation and mutual respect.

"Do not introduce strife into your home!" is a blunt warning from the Talmud.

So important is *shalom bayis* that Jewish law made it an exception to the prohibition of telling a lie, several major Torah sages allowed themselves to be humiliated if it preserved the peacefulness of the home, newlyweds were exempt from serving in the army for the first year, and, it was decided that if a Jew only has enough money to buy either Chanuka candles or Shabbas candles, he must buy the candles for Shabbas because they symbolize *shalom bayis*.

> A young kollel man used to *daven k'vasikin* (with the dawn) on Shabbas mornings. During the summertime, the *minyan* ended early in the morning, so he used to stay in *shul* to learn. One Shabbas morning he was so tired that he fell asleep over his Gemora until 11:00 a.m. When he woke he was shocked to see the time and concerned at what his wife might be thinking, so he started to run home. On the way, he met Rav Shach, who asked, "What's the rush? Are you rushing to the *beis medrash* to learn?"
>
> "No, I fell asleep over my Gemora and I'm running home to make Kiddush."
>
> "You mean your wife has been waiting, not knowing what happened to you? Let me run home with you. For *shalom bayis* let me be the one to explain what happened. Perhaps it'll be easier for her to accept it from me!"

He who establishes harmony in his own home, writes *Avos d'Rabbi Nosson*, "is considered as having established peace in all of Israel!"

But how? How to achieve domestic bliss?

The answer is quite simple: don't! In other words: do all the don'ts!

Don't provoke, don't raise your voice, don't be unforgiving, don't embarrass, don't be inflexible, don't always be right, don't insist on protocol, don't take anything for granted, don't be insensitive, don't make excessive or unrealistic demands, don't be haughty (a man too good for the world is no good for his wife!), don't honor yourself more than your spouse (if your wife is short, bend down so you can hear her whisper!), don't complain over the *cholent* and kugel, don't become an ascetic (love is like butter: it's good with bread!), don't forget affection and sensitivity, don't forget to tell jokes and bring humor into the house, don't forget to appreciate and compliment and chip in…and above all don't forget her birthday!

Why? Because the Jewish wife is the *akeres habayis*, the "foundation of the home," the one who forges the atmosphere of the house ("A person receives blessings only in the merit of his wife!"). Remember: a man is only complete when he takes a wife…and then he's *really* finished!

> The Lubavitcher Rebbe once commented that the difficulty in achieving *shalom bayis* is the best indicator of its vital importance. The Rebbe would always tell his chassidim to set aside some time for their spouses. When the Rebbe was recuperating from his heart attack in 5738, one of his doctors inquired into his daily schedule. The Rebbe told the doctor that when he arrives home, he takes time to sit with the Rebbetzin over a cup of tea and converse. "I suggest," the Rebbe advised the doctor, "that you act in a similar manner when you go home."

"The greater the harmony, mutual respect and devotion between a husband and wife," wrote the seventh Lubavitcher Rebbe, "the greater is the measure of God's blessings to both of them for all their needs!"

The newlywed wife said to her husband when he returned from work, "I have great news for you. Pretty soon, we're going to be three in this house instead of two."

Her husband ran to her with a smile on his face and delight in his eyes.

He was glowing with happiness and kissing his wife when she said, "I'm glad that you feel this way since tomorrow morning, my mother moves in with us."

# Week 42

## On Shame

It's better to be embarrassed than ashamed.
— *Yiddish folk saying*

A wealthy Jerusalemite sent all of his friends, including one named Kamtza, invitations to an elaborate party. However, the invitation intended for Kamtza was accidentally sent to an enemy of the host, a man with a similar name, Bar Kamtza. Surprised to find Bar Kamtza, who had erroneously received an invitation, in his home, the wealthy host ordered him to leave.

But Bar Kamtza pleaded, "Please do not shame me. I even will pay for my meal if you allow me to stay." When the host would not agree, Bar Kamtza then offered to pay for half and then the entire cost of the banquet.

"Under no circumstances," replied the host, who ejected Bar Kamtza.

Bar Kamtza's shame was so great that he sought revenge by telling the Roman procurator Vespasian, "The Jews are about to rebel against you." Believing his words to be true, the Roman official ordered the destruction of the Temple.

# The Name of the Game Is Shame

> A *tzedaka* box was once stolen from the home of Rav Aryeh Leib Alter, the *Sfas Emes*, and one of his employees was suspected of being the thief. When the Gerer Rebbe asked him to return the money, the accused quickly denied stealing it. However, after the Rebbe persisted, the man broke down and confessed. The Rebbe felt sorry for the man because he knew he would be embarrassed to face the other employees after the theft became public knowledge.
>
> "In order to avoid embarrassment," suggested the Rebbe, "why don't you stop coming to work and I will send your salary to your home each month."

Shame began on Day One with Adam and Eve. There was no need for clothes in Eden, and the couple "were not ashamed."

However, once they helped themselves to the Tree of Knowledge, the Rambam points out that the First Couple suddenly hid in the bushes, covered themselves, and experienced the first visible stigma of human shame in the presence of God, the first act of *yiras Shamayim* (fear of Heaven).

The lesson?

Shame and guilt live side by side. In fact, before they discovered how to blush, they had no identity; Adam was simply *ha'adam*, "the man," and Eve was *ha'isha*, "the woman."

With shame, the *ha* is dropped: man becomes Adam, woman becomes Eve. In Eastern Europe there was a saying: Where there's no shame before men, there's no fear of God!

Public humiliation is worse than physical pain, says the Talmud, tantamount to "spilling blood"; *malbin panim* literally means that the open humiliation has "drained the blood from the face."

Even worse, writes the *Ben Ish Chai* in his sefer *Ben Y'hoyada*, the blood is spilled repeatedly because each time one remembers being embarrassed, the shame is felt again.

The *Zohar* puts it this way: you can only kill a man once; but when you shame him, you kill him many times over!

> One morning Rav Simcha Zissel Broide, the *rosh yeshiva* of Chevron, was in the middle of putting on his *tefillin* when a worker in the yeshiva passed him by and wished him a good morning. Rav Simcha Zissel could not respond. However, immediately after he finished putting on his *tefillin*, the

*rosh yeshiva*, concerned the worker might be humiliated by the rejection, went running out of the *beis medrash* to find him and apologize.

The absence of shame, posits Ulla ben Yishmael, is why Jerusalem was destroyed; meanwhile the Midrash suggests, "Don't be ashamed of others; better to be ashamed of yourself!"

"You shall surely reprove your fellow man," says the Torah, but the Talmud quickly adds, "but not if his face will turn red with shame!"

When Yosef meets his brothers after twenty-two years he asks the Egyptians to leave them alone, in order not to embarrass them in front of others; when confronted by the prophet Nosson, David feels shame and remorse for enabling the murder of Batsheva's husband.

> A young man was about to enter military service and was ashamed that he might not be able to fully keep the mitzvos, so he asked the *Chofetz Chaim*, "What shall I do if I can't get kosher food or keep Shabbas?" The *Chofetz Chaim* replied, "The Torah recognizes that there are emergencies. You do not have to starve or put your life in jeopardy by reason of being in the military. If you have to eat *treifa*, eat it — but don't suck the bones. If you have to break Shabbas, do so — but don't enjoy it!" What is the worst punishment for a transgression? That you know you are transgressing, and it gives you no pleasure. And the highest reward for doing a mitzva? That you derive pleasure from doing the right thing.

The thrice-daily Talmud-derived plea in *Shemoneh Esrei*, "We shall not be ashamed," coupled with the prayer said on *Shabbas Mevarchim* (the Shabbas that a new month is announced) to be granted a "life of honor," is a request for honor in the absence of the shame of failure in Torah and mitzvos.

"If you feel shame over having sinned, Heaven immediately forgives you."

Why? Because shame, an awareness of wrongdoing and a desire to do better, is a segue to morality which leads to *teshuva* (return, repentance).

Rabbi Yisroel Salanter Lipkin had a way to avoid embarrassment and shame: "Not everything that is thought should be spoken, not everything that is spoken should be written, and not everything that is written should be printed!"

"You should be ashamed of yourself," the judge said to Bernie, the defendant. "I thought I told you I never wanted to see you in here again!"

"Your Honor," Bernie replies, "that's exactly what I tried to tell the police, but they wouldn't listen!"

# Week 43

## On Showing Gratitude, *Hakoras Hatov*

If a Jew breaks his leg, he thanks God he didn't break both legs; if he breaks both legs, he thanks God he didn't break his neck!

— *Yiddish folk saying*

Rav Shach once asked his grandson to accompany him on a *shiva* call and, despite his fragile health, insisted, "We will go by foot."

The grandson nevertheless called his friend and asked that he cruise by the house. "When you see us coming out the door, drive up and offer my grandfather a ride as though you happen to be going in that direction." Indeed, this is what happened.

On the way Rav Shach asked, "Why do you think I did not want to ask for a ride?"

"Because *zeidy* does not want to trouble anyone."

"True, but let me tell you why I don't want to trouble anyone. Every favor that a person accepts puts him in a debt of *hakoras hatov* which is a tremendous obligation, one that is often never completely satisfied. In my weakened state, I must be especially careful not to accept favors that I no longer have the ability to return!"

# Saying Thanks!

> The Klausenberger Rebbe, Rav Yekusiel Yehuda Halberstam, once entered the *beis medrash* and was disturbed to see a large pile of *seforim* on the table. He called his students together and reminded them that *hakoras hatov* (showing appreciation and gratitude) applies to everything, not just people. "Besides the intrinsic holiness of *seforim*, which demands respect, a student who gains insight from a particular *sefer* must feel gratitude both towards the author and towards the actual book. Therefore, having benefited from a particular *sefer*, one is obligated to show that he appreciates the gain he has received from it by returning it to its proper place!"

In the future, says a Midrash, there'll be no more need for sacrifices — except one: the *korban toda*, the thanksgiving sacrifice, because there'll always be someone to say *thank you* to.

When the Ponevezher Rav visited Cologne, Germany, in 1930, he spent many hours in the home of the city's rabbi, Rav Pinchas Wolfe. While he was there, a button fell off his coat and his hostess, Rebbetzin Wolfe, graciously sewed it back on. Several years later, Reb Yosef Shlomo met up with Rabbi and Rebbetzin Wolfe in Eretz Yisroel and thanked her, again, for sewing on the button — ten years earlier.

Rav Hutner notes that *toda* not only comes from the noun *hoda'a* (thanks), but can also mean "to admit" (i.e., before you give thanks, you must admit to needing something!).

How do we know when the term means *thanks* or *admit*?

Look at the preposition immediately after the word. When *hoda'a* means "to admit," you'll find the conjunction *she* (that); when it means "thanks," it'll be followed by the preposition *al* (concerning).

Here's a perfect example: in the daily thanksgiving prayer, *Modim anachnu lach she…*, the translation is not, "We thank you, God…" but "We admit to you, God [that we are dependent on You]." It's only at the end of the *tefilla*, *after* admitting, that we finally give thanks (*Nodeh lecha u'nesaper tehillasecha al…*).

A Midrash describes the first act of *hakoras hatov*: when asked by God to "Go to Pharaoh and take My people out of *Mitzrayim*," Moshe replied, "I cannot go before I request permission from my father-in-law."

Having been warmly welcomed into Yisro's home, Moshe felt he couldn't just pick up and leave without giving thanks.

> Rav Hillel Kuperman was surprised when Rav Meir Chodosh showed up at his wedding, asking, "Why did you trouble yourself if you're not feeling well?"
>
> The *mashgiach* of Chevron Yeshiva replied, "Don't you remember that you once drove my wife to the hospital?"
>
> "Yes, but if you're not feeling well…"
>
> "Not feeling well does not excuse one from the obligation to show his appreciation!" the *mashgiach* said adamantly.

The ability to recognize kindness appears right in the first of the Ten Commandments; after identifying Himself, God immediately reminds the Jews that "it was I Who took you out of the land of Egypt, out of the house of bondage."

Remember: even God continued to call Moshe by his Egyptian name, in honor of the act of kindness displayed by Pharoah's daughter who saved him from the Nile.

The Chida never forgot a favor. The *Chofetz Chaim*'s rebbe, Nochumke of Horodne, thanked God daily for the sole pair of overalls he owned. Reb Yaakov Kamenetsky's gratitude was evident in his tone and expression.

> Once Reb Yaakov Kamenetsky got out of a car and, distracted for a moment by a greeting from a prominent *rav*, didn't notice the car drive away. Reb Yaakov was so devastated that he made a point of finding the driver's phone number and calling him later to thank him for the ride.

The opposite of being a *makir tov*, "a grateful person," is *kefias tov*. Not being able to recognize and acknowledge the good one receives from others is a contemptible character trait. *Pirkei d'Rabbi Eliezer* asserts that the most despised of all people in God's eyes is the *kafui tov*!

It's human nature, explains Rav Shlomo Wolbe, to take things for granted; however, he reminds us, there are no "givens" in this world and we should not take the goodness we enjoy for granted. Ingratitude to man, Shmuel Hanagid reminded us, "is ingratitude to God!"

Adds Rabba: the wine might belong to the owner but we give thanks to the butler!

Yaakov is in shul one morning praying at his good fortune. He has a wife who is good to him and a home blessed with *shalom bayis*. After thanking God he asks Him, "Tell me, God, why did You make her so kind-hearted?"

"So you could love her," comes the response.

"Tell me, God, why did You make her so good-looking?"

"So you could love her," God answers.

"Why did You make her such a good cook?"

"So you could love her."

"And such a good mother?"

"So you could love her."

Yaakov thinks for a moment, and then continues, "I don't want to sound rude or ungrateful, God, but how come You made her so unintelligent?"

"So she could love you!"

# Week 44

## On Stealing, Returning, Using Lost Objects

*The guilty run even when no one is chasing them!*
— *Yiddish folk saying*

While traveling in a wagon, the *Chofetz Chaim* was engrossed in Torah study when he realized that the wagon had suddenly come to a stop. He looked up to see what was happening and saw that the driver was no longer in his seat but was carrying a pile of hay toward the horse. The driver seemed to be in a tremendous rush to feed the horse so he could drive off right away.

"What have you done?" asked the *Chofetz Chaim*.

"Nothing," replied the driver.

"What do you mean, nothing?"

"I just took some hay for my horse."

"Why don't you say simply say, 'I stole'?"

"Yes, I guess it's sort of stealing."

"No, not 'sort of.' That is outright theft. It makes no difference how you refer to it!"

The *Chofetz Chaim* demanded that the driver return the hay and then said to him, "Perhaps that is why the Torah uses the plural form *lo signovu*, to include all forms of so-called 'petty theft.'"

# A Thief Is a Thief Is a Thief...

> One cold winter evening, Rav Yisroel Salanter and another prominent rabbi arrived at a guesthouse. The rabbi opened the door to let Rav Yisroel go in, but instead he quickly closed it, saying, "While we're trying to decide which one of us should fulfill the mitzva to honor the elderly and let the other enter first, we commit the sin of stealing by leaving the door open and letting the warm air escape!"

When a grandson of a great *talmid chacham* was caught stealing an apple from a basket, Rav Nosson Tzvi Finkel was asked how that was possible.

Perhaps, explained the Alter of Slabodka, the problem began when the impressionable young boy saw his *zeidy* sitting at the back of the *shul* out of an insincere humility (a form of theft, called *geneivas da'as*, "fooling people"), and then perhaps he heard his father give a *d'var* Torah without crediting who he heard it from (another form of theft), and so on, until it was a natural progression for the young grandchild to steal an apple and commit a direct form of theft!

> One day a man dropped in to visit the Steipler Rav to offer his assistance in helping to photocopy some pages. He said he would take them to his office the next day and use the copier there. The Steipler responded harshly. "Did you receive permission from your boss? Are you allowed to use the machine for your personal use? That is stealing!"

The Vilna Gaon says stealing comes in many forms. Moshe Chaim Luzzatto thought wasting another's time was robbery, and the *Chazon Ish* never knocked loudly on someone's door in order to avoid damaging the owner's property (a form of theft).

Abba Yosef was a rabbi and a builder's laborer. One day while he was working, someone came over to him to discuss a matter of Jewish concern. "I am a day laborer," said the rabbi, "and I must not leave my work, so please say what you want quickly and leave."

> One day in B'nei Brak a yeshiva student visiting from Yerushalayim noticed a bag at a bus stop, opened it and was surprised to see it full of cash. After waiting to see if the owner would return he took it home and gave it to his father. The family then mobilized and immediately sent all the children out to put up citywide *hashavas aveida* signs, announcing the lost bag. A few hours later, a man arrived and proved he was the rightful owner. He explained that the money was his savings for an apartment, to be ready when he found a *shidduch* for his daughter. A few weeks later, he called to

say that his wife had heard good things about their son from a *shadchan* and perhaps the children could meet? They did, and were soon engaged.

After outlining the mitzva of returning lost objects the Torah uses the expression "*Lo suchal l'his'alem* (You shall not hide yourself)." This makes it a proactive obligation, in that you can't walk by a lost object that appears to have value and do nothing. Even if it seems useless to you (e.g., a single glove, a family photo), you cannot "hide yourself" from it.

It is assumed that lost articles, especially clothing, have *simanim* (signs of identification) and rightful owners (*tovim*); thus they must be picked up and the find immediately announced to the community.

The obligation starts not when you pick it up, but from the moment you see it!

> One day during the 1948 War of Independence, Rebbetzin Meltzer went to the store to buy some rationed kerosene. She took her place at the end of a long line, but the seller noticed her and, out of respect, filled her jar right away. When Rav Isser Zalman found out he cried out, "That is stealing! You cannot go to the front after others have been waiting patiently! Please return the kerosene immediately and wait in the queue for your ration like everyone else!"

In an early attempt at court liberalism, Yosef ben Chiya suggests, "Not the mouse but the hole is the thief."

His colleague Rabba concurs ("the breach invites the thief!") but Rav Yosef Caro makes it crystal clear: "A thief is a thief is a thief — whether he steals much or little!"

An elderly religious woman returned to her home after an evening of religious service and interrupted an intruder robbing her home. She yelled out the first thing that came to her mind: "Stop! Acts 2:38!" [Turn from your sin]. The burglar immediately stopped dead in his tracks as she calmly called the police. As they handcuffed the burglar, they asked, puzzled, "Why did you just stand there? All the old lady did was yell a Scripture at you…"

"Scripture?" he replied. "She said she had an axe and two 38s!"

# Week 45

## On Supporting Torah Scholars and Institutions

*There is no limit to the good you can do
if you don't care who gets the credit!*

— *Yiddish folk saying*

There is a famous story of how a wealthy Jew offered to pay the full cost of the *Chofetz Chaim*'s new yeshiva only to be surprised by the response. "That is a wonderful offer and Hashem will reward you for your good intentions," replied the *Chofetz Chaim*, "but I must decline. A yeshiva is a public entity, and building a yeshiva is a public mitzva in which every member of a community should participate. We learn this from the building of the *Mishkan*, when Hashem instructed Moshe to collect the money 'from every man.' At that time the Jewish people were so rich that there were probably many individuals who could have paid for the *mishkan* single-handedly. Yet, that was not the will of the *Ribbono shel Olam*, who wanted each and every member of the nation to have a share in building the holy sanctuary." When he spoke at the *chanukas habayis* for his new yeshiva in Radin, the *Chofetz Chaim* reiterated that it was obligatory on "every single Jew in every generation" to participate in building sanctuaries of study and prayer with such a comfortable *ruach* that the *Shechina* will not only visit — but stay!

# Rejoice, Zevulun!

> During the War of 1948 when there was a severe food shortage in Eretz Yisroel, Rav Ezra Attiya, *rosh yeshiva* of Porat Yosef, despite being physically weak, would run around the city looking for food for his students, explaining, "We are not talking only about a shortage of food but also about the shortage of Torah learning that comes about as a result. Who will be responsible for this reduction in Torah learning if not those who were able to do something about it and did not?"

It doesn't come by inheritance!

Those are the words of *Pirkei Avos*. Torah, they remind us, requires sweat, labor, determination, focus and hard work — or at least, indirect support.

The Manchester Gaon, Rav Yehuda Zev Segal, always got up early to make sure he turned on the lights in the *beis medrash* so he felt that he contributed towards everyone else's learning throughout the day.

According to Rabbi Acha, "Even if one has learned and taught Torah but failed to promote Torah among others when he had the opportunity to do so, he is included in the Torah's curse. Conversely, if one strengthens Torah in his circles, he is included in the Torah's blessing — even, incredibly, if he doesn't personally learn Torah or observe its mitzvos!"

This is startling: an irreligious Jew is blessed if he simply *supports* Torah without learning Torah!

In another stunning interpretation, Rabbi Eleazar takes the verse "*V'rav shalom banayich* (And great shall be the peace of your children [*banayich*])," and translates the word *banayich* as *bonayich*, "your builders," implying that it is the "*builders* of Torah," and not the *students* of Torah, who are blessed with peace.

> A *rosh kollel* once came to Rabbi Yehuda Tzadka, *rosh yeshiva* of Porat Yosef, to request his approbation for republishing certain *seforim* written in previous centuries. Rabbi Tzadka agreed, but added, "You should know that providing for the members of your *kollel* is an even greater *mitzva* than publishing these *seforim*." Rav Tzadka was dismayed that more and more *seforim* were being published but the number of learners was diminishing.

The mitzva to support Torah learning is derived from the example of the tribe of Zevulun donating half of its profits to the tribe of Yissachar, who were studying Torah. Their purpose? To become equal partners in the reward for keeping Torah alive.

Zevulun settled near the harbor to take advantage of the commerce, while Yissachar's members chose to be indoors undisturbed, studying Torah: "Rejoice, Zevulun, in your excursions and Yissachar in your tents [of study]."

Why include "excursions" in the blessing?

Those who travel on business study less Torah, and less study means less of the protection that Torah study provides. Thus a more accurate reading would be, "Rejoice, Zevulun, in your excursions, *because* Yissachar is in the tents [of study]!"

Rav Chaim Volozhiner compares this cushion of security to a tall tree rooted in the middle of a deep ocean with raging waters. Those who grip the tree survive; others drown. Similarly, Jews who support the Torah tree will not only survive Jewishly but will even be blessed *before* Yissachar (whose name appears second in the *bracha*).

> Whenever Rav Shneur Kotler went to parlor meetings to fundraise, he would never specifically ask for money for his Lakewood Yeshiva but simply spoke about the need to support all Torah institutions in general. After one wedding where Rav Shneur Kotler was *mesader kiddushin*, the father of the *chassan* gave him a check as was the custom. Several weeks later, they met at another *simcha* and the father said, "I was a bit disappointed to see that you endorsed my check to the yeshiva when I intended it for you to use for your personal needs."
>
> "*Oy*, what a pity," Rav Shneur replied, "If I had known the money was meant for me and not the yeshiva I would have given it to *chinuch atzmai* [the independent chareidi school system in Eretz Yisroel]!"

There is no specific mitzva in putting up *batei medrashim* nor *batei kenessiyos*, but these places are considered miniature "sanctuaries" in exile (*mikdashei me'at*). That is why King Solomon purposefully built his *Beis Hamikdash* from wood, a material that inevitably decays over time, thus acting as a reminder to each future generation to be involved in its reconstruction.

Every morning when Rav Avigdor Miller would walk past the Mir in Brooklyn, he would repeat a little prayer: "May the *rosh yeshiva* [Rav Shmuel Berenbaum] be blessed, may the *bochurim* be blessed…" in gratitude for having such *talmidei chachamim* in the neighborhood.

The *rav* and his wife were cleaning the house before Pesach when the *rav* found a box he didn't recognize. The rebbetzin said it was personal and he should leave it alone; she would take care of cleaning it for Pesach. But the *rav* couldn't contain his curiosity so when his wife wasn't looking, he opened the box. Inside he found three eggs and two thousand dollars. When the rebbetzin came home, the *rav* admitted that he had opened the box and asked her to explain its contents.

"Well," she explained, "it was my way of following your *divrei Torah*. Whenever you gave a bad sermon I put an egg in the box."

"Wow!" he thought, "in twenty years, only three bad sermons! That's not bad!"

"And," continued the rebbetzin, "every time I got a dozen eggs, I would sell them for a dollar!"

# Week 46

## On Taking Advantage of Another Person

A favor costs the favored dearly.
— *Yiddish folk saying*

The Gerer Rebbe, Rav Avraham Mordechai Alter, was famous for making every effort not to trouble others. As long as he was able to take care of his own affairs he never asked anyone else for help. When the Rebbe became elderly and his health deteriorated, a few men were appointed to work in shifts to tend to his needs. Even then, the Rebbe hesitated to ask for help. He expressed great appreciation for everything they did on their own and was always concerned about their well-being. The Rebbe wanted to make sure that those helping him were not working too hard or losing sleep on his account.

On one particular occasion, the Rebbe was eating lunch while a group of children sat around his table. When he finished eating, he got up from his seat to wash his hands for *bensching* and returned to his seat. The rebbetzin noticed that he had gotten up and said, "Why didn't you just ask one of the children to bring you some water? It is important to educate them."

"Indeed," said the Rebbe, "educating children is very important, and that is exactly what I was doing. I want them to know that 'What you can do on your own, do not trouble others to do!'"

# Stepping on Toes

> Rav Nosson Tzvi Finkel, the Alter of Slabodka, didn't like to see his students rushing into the *beis medrash* pushing each other trying to get a seat in the front, especially when one student ousted another from his rightful place. So he gave a *drasha*: "When *Hashem* created the trees, they did not race into their positions forcefully but grew peacefully and steadily in their own positions, each one at a distance from the other so as not to infringe on the other's space. Seeing this, the grass made a *kal v'chomer*: If, regarding the trees that need their own space in order for their leaves to grow nicely, *Hashem* said, '*l'minehu*, each for itself,' then we, the grass, that are meant to grow in clusters, must certainly be careful that we contain ourselves within our own spaces." "So," concluded the Alter, "we are a group of students who are meant to be together, and we must learn a *kal v'chomer* from the grass: If the grass was careful not to 'step on the other's toes,' then certainly yeshiva students, who are obligated to honor one another, must be careful to give each other the space they need!"

This sensitivity of "not intruding" even applies to giving credit to the wrong person for a quote. And in reverse: quoting correctly "brings redemption to the world, as it is written, 'And Esther said to the king *in the name of* Mordechai.'"

Thus if you say words of Torah and credit Rabbi Eliezer when in fact they were spoken by Rabbi Yehoshua, you have "trespassed." This is why so many people use the generic term *chazal* (*chachameinu zichronam livracha*, "our Sages of blessed memory"), which refers to sages and Torah scholars in general.

> Whenever Rabbi Reuven Bengis learned in the *beis medrash*, he sat with a full cup of tea in front of him, which he would not drink. Why? He knew that many of those who passed by his place in the *beis medrash* would stop and ask him if he would like a hot drink. Since he didn't want to trouble others on his account, he always placed a cup of tea in front of his *sefer*. And it was always a full cup just in case someone offered a refill!

Rabbeinu Yona would not ask a favor from anybody unless he was absolutely convinced it was not an imposition. Rabbi Nissim Karelitz thought it improper for husbands to ask their wives to clean more for Pesach than the wives thought necessary.

Rav Yehuda Tzadka once went to the doctor's office and found a long line of people waiting. The doctor recognized the respected *rav* and called him to enter the office ahead of the others, but Rav Yehuda declined to do so, insisting on waiting his turn.

Rav Bentzion Abba Shaul was so sensitive about not being a burden on others (*ish b'achiv lo sirde bo b'forech*) that he would clean his house before the cleaning woman came. In his yeshiva, he once yelled at a *bochur* for leaving orange peels on the window sill because it showed inconsideration towards the janitor.

Even after he became the rebbe, Rav Simcha Bunim would go to his neighbor and borrow pliers to make home repairs. Rav Simcha preferred to do what he could by himself rather than have to trouble others.

> The *Chazon Ish* would not ask for something if he felt the other person would be "compelled to comply." And in a famous letter, he begs his followers that they "not bog me down with requests that I cannot or am opposed to fulfilling [...for] to ask someone to do something that he cannot do is a breach of '*lo sirde bo b'forech*.' ...Do not say to yourself, 'Where is the harm in asking?' There is definite harm done when one asks for a favor that is too difficult to grant!"

Misleading others is a crime.

The Torah warns, "*V'lifnei iver lo sitein michshol* (You shall not place a stumbling block before the blind)."

What does this mean? You cannot take advantage of someone's "blindness" (i.e., ignorance) and mislead them. Thus you cannot offer a glass of wine to a *nazir* (after he has sworn off drink), nor lend money with interest to one who doesn't know that it's forbidden.

Let's give the final word to *Peninei Hamelitzos*: If you do a man a favor, you will be his superior; if you get one from him, his inferior; if you do not need him at all, his friend!

A shnorrer manages to get an appointment with a wealthy Jewish philanthropist by insisting that he has a foolproof way for the man to make five hundred thousand dollars.

"So let me hear your great idea," the philanthropist says.

"It's very simple. I understand that when your daughter gets married you're planning on giving her a dowry of a million dollars."

"Nu?"

"So, I've come to tell you that I'm willing to marry her — for half the amount!"

# Week 47

## On Teaching Torah to Others

> Only a fool grows without rain.
> — *Yiddish folk saying*

A pious *shochet* once wanted to change his occupation to a *cheder* teacher, so he asked Rav Yisroel Salanter for advice, complaining that the responsibility in his current job was too great. Rav Yisroel's response was that teaching children is a much greater responsibility than supplying kosher meat to the public. A teacher molds his students into people who will eventually have their own children. "Your actions can have an everlasting effect from generation to generation."

# The Joy of Torah Is Torah

> The Steipler used to say that a rebbe's personal conduct usually has more of an impact on his students than his teachings. If a young student sees his rebbe, his spiritual mentor, reciting a *bracha* with *kavana*, then he will learn to follow his example. The Steipler also suggested that *rabbeim* spice their teachings with short anecdotes and lessons that inspire *yiras Shamayim*.
>
> A Jew once told the Steipler that all his life he had always steered clear from even the slightest hint of deceit or theft. This was because, when he was a young boy, his *cheder* rebbe repetedly said to his class, "Please learn well; otherwise you will make me into a thief! Your fathers pay me to teach you!"

Rebbi Meir said, "He who learns Torah, and fails to share it with other people, falls into the category of cheapening the Word of God." *Tanna d'Vei Eliyahu* adds: such a person will eventually forget his own Torah wisdom!

It's human nature: if you learn something knowing in advance that you have to explain it to a third person, your learning is more focused, more concentrated. And more: all mitzvos must be directed at others, as exemplified by Avraham's behavior.

If you learn Torah, says Rabbi Akiva, and do not teach it, you "scorn the word of God!" Adds the Mishna, "If you teach others, your own wisdom will increase and be increased upon!"

And in reverse: "If one has learned Torah but does not provide others with the same opportunity, he brings evil upon himself [for eventually] his own Torah knowledge will diminish!"

> Rav Moshe Rosenstein, the *mashgiach* of the Lomzeh Yeshiva, was sitting and learning *chumash* with a young boy.
>
> "Who is that boy to whom the *mashgiach* is dedicating so much time?" a *chaver* asked Rav Moshe.
>
> The *mashgiach* whispered back with a smile, "He is the son of *HaKadosh Boruch Hu*! Do you think only the children of the elite deserve special attention? Is the fact that he is *Hashem*'s dear child not enough reason that I should learn with him?"

The Mishna is not impressed if you "have learned much Torah" if you don't go out and teach others what you've learned.

Rav Shach extended the usual understanding of the *pasuk* "You shall not take the name of *Hashem* in vain" as applying to those who learn Torah but are negligent in teaching it.

There's nothing more fruitless than to learn and not teach, Rabbi Yose ben Chalafta taught his students, quoting a Midrash: "Those who learn for the purpose of teaching receive inspiration!"

And the rewards are better! "He who learns receives but one-fifth of the reward that goes to one who teaches," is a midrashic take on *Shir Hashirim*.

> A poor man came to see the Kobriner Rebbe complaining that he couldn't sustain his learning. "Why not?" asked the Rebbe.
> "Because the urge to do evil constantly throws me off course. What am I to do?"
> "Excuse me, but do you know how to ride a horse?"
> "Absolutely!"
> "And how do you respond when you fall off your horse?"
> "Well, I get back on. What else is a man to do?"
> "So," replied the Kobriner, a masterful teacher, "think of the *yetzer hora* as your horse. When you fall off, get back on. As you have said, 'What else is a man supposed to do?' Soon you will be the horse's master!"

But don't get too arrogant in teaching, advises the Mishna; "If you have learned much Torah, do not take credit for yourself, because that is what you were created to do!" And remember, adds Rashi: teachers learn from their students.

When he saw young promising students "at risk," the *Chofetz Chaim* called them "boys who could have become Torah leaders but instead grew into uneducated men because of the lack of [dedicated] Torah teachers [without whom] the Torah would lie in a corner, and remain hidden from the generation!"

What is more worthy, explains the *Midrash Shmuel*, is going out and teaching, helping others grow in Torah as well. Those who learn for the purpose of teaching, says a Midrash, receive "inspiration."

Rav Mordechai Gifter's favorite mantra was: "The joy of Torah is inherently Torah!

The *rosh yeshiva* was scheduled to speak at an important Torah convention, so he asked his staff to write him an insightful, humorous twenty-minute *d'var Torah*. When he returned to the yeshiva, he was furious.

"What happened?! It took me an hour to say the speech! Half the audience walked out before I finished!"

"An hour?" one baffled employee replied. "We wrote you a twenty-minute speech…and I also gave you the two extra copies you asked for."

# Week 48

## On Time Management

Sleep faster, we need the pillows!
— *Yiddish folk saying*

The *shul shammas* returned from his first visit to the big city and brought one of the exciting inventions of that time, a clock.

The rabbi in his tiny village was fascinated when the *shammas* told him that the clock's function was to tell time, for example when to have one's daily meals. Thus, he explained, when it pointed in the morning to six, it was breakfast time; at twelve noon it was time to eat lunch; and in the evening, suppertime came when the clock pointed to eight.

But the rabbi was unimpressed, saying that he wouldn't let some newfangled device tell him when to eat his meals.

The *shammas* smiled and agreed, "We are not such fools as to let a piece of metal tell us when to eat. No, when I am hungry in the morning, I will set the clock for six; and when I want to eat lunch, I will push the hand to twelve; and likewise when I feel like having my third meal."

# Well, It's about Time!

The time it took for Rav Avraham Mordechai of Ger to get out of bed, get dressed and go downstairs was a matter of seconds. He would button his jacket as he walked towards his study because every second was precious. During a two-hour recess in an important meeting at Lodz, the Rebbe managed to eat lunch, attend a ceremony to complete a *sefer Torah* and its *seudas mitzva* where he gave *divrei Torah* and parceled "*shirayim*" (leftovers from the Rebbe's food). Afterwards, he went to visit two Gerer Chassidim who were ill and also attended a *sheva brachos*. Then he stopped off at a meeting of philanthropists discussing charitable undertakings in Eretz Yisroel. Finally, the Rebbe went back to the original meeting and arrived several minutes early, being the first one there.

The Gerer Rebbe hired a man to come to his house every morning at a set hour to wake him up to learn Torah. One morning, because the Rebbe was very tired, he did not hear the man's knock at the door, and, as a result, he rose a few minutes later than usual. The few minutes of Torah learning that he had lost was a source of tremendous anguish for the Rebbe, and he begged the man who was responsible for waking him up to have no mercy on him in the future and to knock on the door very loudly. In fact, years later, when the two met again, the Rebbe still expressed remorse over the lost minutes that morning.

"I ask of all my chassidim," said Reb Menachem Mendel of Kotzk, "When you are confronted by the *yetzer hora* and he wishes to con you into committing a sin, do not listen to him. Not because you oppose his advice, but because you simply don't have the time to listen to his enticement!"

Rav Zelig Braverman's motto was: "If you have time, nothing gets done, but if you're under pressure for time, you can achieve worlds!"

The Gerer Rebbe was so punctual that one could set his watch according to the Rebbe's movements. On one occasion, a full minute went by after the Rebbe's usual time of arrival and there was no sign of him. Rav Bunim Leibel, the Rebbe's anxious assistant, was sent to inquire after his welfare. When Rav Bunim entered the study, the Rebbe conceded that his watch had just stopped, and he hurried immediately to the *beis medrash* to pray.

The *Sfas Emes* was once invited to attend a meeting at the home of the great sage Rav Elimelech of Grudzisk. When he arrived, all the other rebbes were already seated around the table. The Gerer Rebbe entered the room and said, "My presence was requested at this meeting because of the desperate need to raise 300,000 rubles for the upkeep of our schools. Therefore, I accept upon myself the responsibility of raising 100,000 rubles, and I ask the rebbes of Grudzinsk and Alexander to raise 50,000 each. The rebbes of Sochotshov, Porisov, Radomsk and Skarnovitz are asked to raise 25,000. Is that acceptable?"

The rebbes replied yes, so the Gerer Rebbe said good-bye and made his way to the door. When the host, Rav Elimelech, asked him to stay for the meal, the Rebbe, unwilling to offend, rushed to wash his hands, went to the table, ate for a few minutes, *bensched* and said good-bye. No more than seven minutes elapsed from the time he entered the house until he left.

When Rav Avraham Mordechai Alter once showed up to meet a certain *gadol*, he was exactly on time but his friend arrived a few minutes later.

"I apologize for the delay," said the other Rebbe, "I was preoccupied with something 'above time.'"

"Perhaps you mean 'below time,'" came the response from the *Imrei Emes*, "for there is nothing more important than time. Time is the most precious commodity we have, and one who cannot deal with time is 'below time'!"

The Tchebiner Rav, Rav Dov Berish Weidenfeld, described the Gerer Rebbe as being "above time," in that what the Rebbe was able to accomplish in short periods of time was almost supernatural. As the Rebbe said, "It is my desire to do God's will, not that God do my will!"

The *Imrei Emes* exemplified the epitome of quick and enthusiastic zealousness (*zerizus*) in *avodas Hashem*; or in modern scientific terms: Time Management.

Even today, a Gerer bris must start on time and last no longer than twenty minutes, including the *seudas mitzva*, singing, *divrei Torah*, *bensching* — and the *bris* itself!

Moishie had this problem of getting up late in the morning and was always late for work. His boss was mad at him and threatened to fire him if he didn't do something about it. So Moishie went to his doctor, who gave him a pill and told him to take it before he went to bed. Moishie slept well, and in fact, beat the alarm in the morning. Moishie had a leisurely breakfast and drove cheerfully to work.

"Boss," Moishie said, "The pill actually worked!"

"That's great!" said the boss, "but where were you yesterday?"

# Week 49

## On Torah as a Protective Umbrella

*In God we trust; all others are suspects!*
— *Yiddish folk saying*

Two of Rabbi Chanina's students were on their way to chop wood when they met an astronomer who gazed at the stars and told them they would die. As they continued walking they met a poor elderly man who begged, "Please, give me something to eat, I haven't eaten in three days." They generously gave him half the bread they had with them. Overjoyed, he blessed them, "May you live a long life, for you have revived me!"

On their way home the Torah students bumped into the stargazer. "How is it possible?" he said. "You're still alive?"

The amazed astronomer searched their belongings and found a snake among their timber that they had unwittingly squashed when they took out the bread for the beggar. When told, the astronomer exclaimed, "What can I do if the God of the Jewish people decided to spare your lives because of a half a loaf of bread!"

# And Students Are Its Towers!

> The Ponovezher Rav once asked the *Chazon Ish* if the yeshiva should insure their building against fire. The *Chazon Ish* said no, as long as Reb Eliezer was present, the yeshiva was safe from harm. Years went by and no harm befell the yeshiva. However, one week after Reb Eliezer passed away, a fire broke out in the yeshiva, causing considerable damage. Who was Reb Eliezer? A survivor of the Kelm Yeshiva, Reb Eliezer had positioned himself at the back of the Ponovezh *beis medrash* and learned Torah day and night. He completed the entire *masechtos Shabbas* and *Eiruvin* (by heart) every *Shabbas*. Reb Eliezer never lay down on a bed, but sat and learned Torah. Every once in a while he would rest his head on his cane and doze off for a few minutes. When he awoke again, he continued right where he left off. He was the Ponovezher Yeshiva's insurance policy!

"The more Torah, the more life!" is Hillel's battle cry.

Torah? It's "a life-given medicine for all Israel," adds Yehuda ben Chiya.

Remember: if only fifty righteous people had been found in Sodom, the city would have been spared! Why? "Torah shields the whole world and acts as a city's ramparts," says Yochanan ben Nappacha, adding, "…and students are its towers!"

Torah scholars, in the eyes of the *Chofetz Chaim*, were "the pillars that support the world."

> Prior to the Six-Day War, when Yerushalayim was in great danger, Rabbi Yehuda Tzadka chose ten of the wisest men in his yeshiva to devote themselves to non-stop Torah learning, explaining,. "If ten righteous people in the wicked city of Sodom could have spared destruction, therefore, if these ten people devote their attention to Torah, they can protect the entire generation!"

"We honor not the commandments but the Commander," writes Rambam, because He "saved us from groping in the dark." Yirmiah ben Eleazar is convinced: a house where Torah is studied at night will not be ruined by day!

Torah, says the *Yismach Yisroel*, is the sole antidote defense to the *yetzer hora*. And if the antidote doesn't work? That means your Torah learning is faulty!

> In 1981, the prime minister of Israel, Menachem Begin, ordered a raid on Iraq's nuclear reactors which successfully knocked out Iraq's nuclear capability against Israel. Prior to the attack, the prime minister telephoned both

the Bava Sali and Rav Shach to inform them of the impending attack and to ask for their prayers.

"What time is the attack to take place?" the Bava Sali asked the prime minister.

"The F-16 planes are to take off at 2 p.m.," replied Mr. Begin.

The Bava Sali then suggested that the raid be postponed to later in the afternoon, which was done, because he wanted it timed to when yeshiva students were back in the *beis medrash* so that the power of their Torah study would protect everyone involved in the mission.

There is a principle that God never sends a malady without a remedy.

When Yaakov sends Yehuda ahead to Goshen *l'horos*, literally "to point the way," Rashi links *l'horos* with Torah. Yehuda was being told to establish a *beis medrash* in advance of the family's arrival. Here, amidst persecution, they had a "safe house" to immerse themselves in Torah study.

> Every man has three friends: his children, his money and his mitzvos/*gemilus chasadim* (good deeds).
>
> When the time comes for him to leave the world he calls upon his children, who reply, "Don't you know that no one can conquer death?"
>
> Then he calls upon his money, saying, "Day and night I have worked for you; save me now."
>
> The money replies, "Wealth cannot deliver you from death!"
>
> He next calls on his mitzvos/*gemilus chasadim* and they reply, "Go in peace! By the time you arrive in the next world, we will be there before you to offer you help!"

"A person who walks his path in life without regard to the Torah's ethical standards," writes Moshe Chaim Luzzatto, "is like a blind man who does not know his journey is along the bank of a river. The dangers of one wrong step and the odds are more in favor of his being hurt than escaping harm!"

After each *shiur* he gave in Slabodka, Reb Yechezkel Abramsky would remind his students, "You boys who spend all of your time learning Torah without any disturbance provide security for all of *Klal Yisroel*!"

Rabbi to a six-year-old boy in his class: "So I hear your mother tucks you into bed every night and even says your prayers for you. That's very commendable. What does she say?"

Little boy: "Thank God he's in bed!"

# Week 50

## On *Tzedaka*

God is not rich; all He does is take
from one and give to the other!

— *Yiddish folk saying*

Rabbi Ezra Attia, *rosh yeshiva* of Porat Yosef, always made sure not to live beyond his means. When it came to basic necessities, Rav Ezra begged his children not to buy their groceries on credit or borrow money. One day Rav Ezra's youngest son, Dovid, was shocked when the local grocer asked him to remind his father that his bill was overdue. "How could it be?" Dovid asked himself, "that my father had an account with the grocer, and how can it be that it was not paid?

Dovid later discovered that the account his father had opened at the grocer was not for himself but for a needy family in the community. He told the grocer not to charge the family for what they bought and that he would pay their bill at the end of each month. This arrangement went on secretly for a long time until R' Atiya fell ill and could no longer personally pay the bill.

# If You Give, You Get!

The Sanzer Rebbe, Rav Chaim Halberstam, although utterly poverty-stricken, disbursed money to the poor like a baron. A gifted fundraiser, the Rebbe supported hundreds of impoverished families and married off orphaned boys and girls always in a discreet, respectful manner. So many people flowed in and out of the Rebbe's house that it was hard to tell who was coming to give and who to get! Giving *tzedaka* was a source of energy for him, and, when the money ran out, the Rebbe would borrow, leaving his personal belongings as collateral. One day a follower told the Rebbe that the wife of a Jew he gives money to was seen buying an expensive duck. "I'm glad you told me that," replied the Rebbe, "I had assumed that he was used to a more modest lifestyle and therefore I only gave him a modest stipend. Now that you say he has expensive taste, I can see that his needs are greater, and I must see to it that he gets more!"

There's a strange old saying: "*Tzadikim* cherish their money more than themselves!" *Tzadikim*, explains Rav Eliyahu Dessler, are more acutely aware than others that they are simply custodians of God's assets.

If *tzadikim* have more money, it's for one reason only: to perform more mitzvos. If they don't share it with the poor, they consider that they are stealing from the poor!

The only fortune that one truly possesses, notes Rabbi Yosef Dov Soloveitchik (the *Beis Halevi*), is the one he has given away to charity.

When asked how much money he had, Baron Rothschild of Frankfurt replied, "The only secure wealth that I have is what I have given to *tzedaka*, as nobody can take that away from me. The rest is not real wealth; it can vanish in a flash!"

One of the most famous palindromes in the Torah (it means the same forwards and backwards) is the Hebrew word *v'nasnu* (and you shall give), meaning, if you give, you get!

Thus, to tithe is not to give but to receive!

From the compound verb *aser te'aser* we get "*aser bishvil sh'tis'asher* (tithe so that you will become rich)!" This is a challenge from God: "Test Me, if you will!"

The question is obvious: Why then are there any poor, generous Jews?

The *Chofetz Chaim* claims that if they didn't become wealthy it was because they gave less than they could!

Rav Chanoch Karelenstein tithed the word *te'aser* (a tenth). A tenth of *taf* was forty; a tenth of *ayin* was seven; a tenth of *shin* was thirty; a tenth of *reish* was twenty.

He then converted these numbers back into Hebrew letters and got *mazalcha*… "your mazel"!

> The Kapishnitzer Rebbe (who would beg God, "Please give money to those with *seichel* [to give] or give *seichel* to those with money!"), would never let *tzedaka* money that his chassidim gave him stay in his house overnight. Since it wasn't his, the Rebbe wanted to give it out as quickly as possible. He always made sure to give it away on the same day. One evening he complained to his *gabbai*, "I have money to distribute to *tzedaka* and no one has come to ask me for it." He then had an idea and wrote a check for the amount made out to *tzedaka* and "in that way it will be considered as if I already gave it!" When he moved from Vienna to the United States, the Rebbe would say that nothing had changed in his life except "in Vienna I dealt in shillings and in America I deal in dollars!"

Remember: if someone asks you for food and you give them clothes, *it's not charity*! If they ask you for a place to sleep, and you give them food, *it's not charity*! If they ask you for clothes, and you give them a bed for the night, *it's not charity*!

"If a poor man does not have clothing, clothe him," writes the Rambam. "If he lacks household utensils, buy them for him. If he does not have a wife, find him a suitable one. If he is used to riding a horse then don't buy him a donkey!"

Hillel once provided a horse and servant for a poor man who was raised in an affluent home. One day the servant was not available, so Hillel himself walked before the horse, leading it for three miles!

A *rosh yeshiva*, known for his lengthy sermons, noticed a man get up and leave during the middle of his *d'var Torah* on *tzedaka*. He came back twenty minutes later near the end of the speech. Afterwards the *rosh yeshiva* asked the man where he had gone.

"I went to get a haircut."

"Why didn't you do that before my speech?"

"Because, I didn't need one back then."

# Week 51

## On Work

When food is lacking in the pantry, quarrel knocks on the door.
— *Yiddish folk saying*

"Greater is one who benefits from the work of his hands than he who stands in fear of Heaven," notes Rabbi Chiya ben Ami; and, "If you eat by the work of your hands," sang King David, "happy are you!"

And not just in this world, as Rabbi Chanina ben Dosa discovered, but "it will also go well for you in the World to Come!"

"Rather skin a carcass for a fee in the market," Rav urged his student Rabbi Kahana, "than be supported by charity. Do not say, 'I am a priest' or 'I am a great man and it is beneath my dignity!'"

And so Rabbi Yehuda would go to the *beis medrash* bearing a pitcher on his shoulders, saying, "Great is labor, for it honors the person who does it!"

# My Son, the Thief!

> "A person must not depend on the work of his ancestors," reminds *Midrash Tehillim*. "If a person does not do good in his lifetime, he cannot fall back on the work of those who came before him. No person will eat in the Time to Come of his parent's work, but only of his own!"

"By the sweat of your brow shall you eat bread!" Who said this? None other than God Himself!

When the manna fell in the desert, Jews were told, "*V'yotzo ha'am v'loktu d'var yom b'yomo* (Go out and pick each day's portion on its day)."

This specific wording, explains Rashi, is the foundation of *bitachon* (faith) in what tomorrow may bring. Those who worry about the next day, says the Maharal, do not fully appreciate what they have today!

This of course is no excuse not to work. Remember: faith alone doesn't pay the rent nor feed the kids.

"How awesome are the works of the Almighty" has led many a Torah sage to delve fully into God's universe to explore the wisdom, beauty and majesty of God. And so the Rambam studied science and medicine, Hillel was an architect, the Vilna Gaon studied maths, and the *Chazon Ish* hired private tutors to teach him agriculture and astronomy.

This was Rabban Gamliel's insight on learning and working: "If the study of Torah is not integrated with work, study will finally be avoided, and thus the absence of work becomes the cause of doing wrong!"

> Rabbi Chanina ben Dosa, at his wife's behest, prayed that he and his family be adequately sustained through the mercy of Heaven. His prayers were answered when he mysteriously discovered a golden pillar whose sale would support them for many years. Soon thereafter Rabbi Chanina saw himself in dream where he sat among the saintly and pious of all ages around golden tables. To his shock, his table was absent a prop, the very golden pillar that was bequeathed to support his family. Though his petition was just, his stake in Paradise was diminished nonetheless. Again at his wife's behest, he prayed that the golden pillar be returned to Heaven. They would live in hunger and want rather than compromise their eternal rewards in the hereafter!

The paradox of learning or working comes from the contradiction between two famous verses.

Between constant Torah study ("This book of Torah shall not depart from your mouth") versus working for a living ("You shall gather your grains, wine, oil"), Rabbi Shimon bar Yochai argues for the former; however Rabbi Yishmael, who lived in the generation following the destruction of the Second Temple, takes a pragmatic position, convinced that having a livelihood is better than being dependent on charity.

Who is right?

Rabbi Yishmael is, according to the rabbis of the Talmud, who admit that things didn't work out so well for those who followed Rabbi Shimon's advice.

The Talmud prefers a rational balance. "Torah not accompanied by work," warns *Pirkei Avos*, "ultimately will be nullified and cause sin."

Adds the *Shulchan Aruch*: "After morning seder, a man should go to work, for Torah without work is destined to be annulled and encourages wrongdoing.... Even a respected Torah scholar who becomes impoverished should engage in a trade, even an undignified one, and not become dependent on others!"

> The Lithuanian *rosh yeshiva* in England was visited by a student who was obviously in a state of panic. "What's wrong?" asked the *rav*.
>
> "I'm leaving the yeshiva and going to study at university," the boy replied. The *rosh yeshiva* shouted at him that he was going astray, reprimanded him bitterly and, as the shocked boy left his office, asked, "By the way, where are you going to study?"
>
> "At Cambridge," answered the student in a weak voice.
>
> "At least at Cambridge!" shouted the rabbi.

Wealth is no sin and work is a source of independence and dignity.

Remember: God "worked" to create the world, and Man needs meaningful work to continue what God started.

When Rabban Gamliel ben Yehuda recommended the study of Torah with *derech eretz* (literally, "the way of the world"), he meant it as a euphemism for employment — for when pursued in tandem, or as the Rambam puts it, *shvil hazahav*, the "golden mean" (i.e., in moderation), then both are strengthened!

To summarize: it is a mitzva to acquire a profession, so much so that a father can teach his children an *umanus* (way of making a living), according to the Rambam and *Shulchan Aruch*, even on a Shabbas!

And if, warns Rashi, you don't teach your children an honest trade, don't be surprised if they grow up to be...thieves!

An Israeli manufacturer is showing his machine factory to a potential customer from Albania. At noon, when the lunch whistle blows, two thousand men and women immediately stop work and leave the building.

"Your workers, they're escaping!" cries the visitor. "You've got to stop them."

"Don't worry, they'll be back," says the Israeli. And indeed, at exactly one o'clock the whistle blows again, and all the workers return from their break. When the tour is over, the Israeli manufacturer turns to his guest and says, "Well, now, which of these machines would you like to order?"

"Forget the machines! How much do you want for that whistle?"

# Week 52

## On Zealousness

*Those who take revenge destroy their own house!*
— *Yiddish folk saying*

When he heard that the wedding of an impoverished couple was about to be canceled due to financial difficulties, Rabbi Yechezkel Abramsky, *av beis din* of London, quickly raised the money needed, put it in an envelope and rushed off to the post office.

Rabbi Y.M. Gordon, the *rosh yeshiva* of Lomzeh, was amazed at Rav Yechezkel's alacrity and asked why he was so eager to personally mail the envelope.

Rav Yechezkel replied with a story about the Vilna Gaon's wife, who made an agreement with her friend that whoever preceded the other to the World to Come would return and tell what went on in *Olam ha'Emes* (the World of Truth). Thirty days after the rebbetzin's friend passed away, she appeared. "Do you remember the day we went out together to raise money for *tzedaka* and we saw a wealthy lady crossing the street and motioned to her to wait for us? And she did, and gave us a nice donation? Well, even the motion that we made towards this woman is written down in the Book of Good."

Rav Yechezkel Abramsky continued, "If every motion that one makes for a mitzva is written down in Heaven, then I certainly want to be the one to prepare the money order and mail it off. I wouldn't want to pass up this great mitzva by having a messenger do it for me instead!"

# Rush Hour

> The *Chofetz Chaim* asked a family member to help him inspect some of his newly printed *seforim*. "Not right now," the man responded. "Later tonight! I'll have more time and I'll even check a hundred *seforim*!"
>
> That evening, when he returned to his room, he found a pile of a hundred *seforim* on his desk. "What's going on here?" he asked.
>
> "If you talk," the *Chofetz Chaim* reminded him, "you must be prepared to do!"

Reb Moshe Chaim Luzzatto equates zealousness not to rage and fury but to "caution."

It's not a question of whether *zerizus* is a mitzva; it is, but only at the right time, in the right place, for the right cause, by the right person.

In the Temple, "an always blazing fire was kept on the altar, never to go out"; but this scorched passion was only available for the few who knew when and why to use it.

One such Jew was Pinchas ben Elazar, an *oheiv shalom v'rodef shalom* (a person seeking to restore peace by making things proper, literally "a lover of peace and a pursuer of peace"). Pinchas's zealousness of double homicide was rewarded with a *bris shalom* (covenant of peace), and a permanent priesthood.

But what did his act of murder achieve?

It put a brake on God's "flaming anger," which was triggered by the sight of the women of Moav seducing Jews into idolatry. By protecting Israel from God's wrath in the form of a catastrophic plague, Pinchas's zeal had "atoned for all Israel"!

Stunningly, the rabbis of the Talmud (Yehuda ben Pazi) say that had it been their decision, they would have thrown Pinchas into *cherem* (rabbinical ban). Why? Because he acted not "by the will of the Sages"!

> The *Chazon Ish* was for demonstrations but against the use of physical force. He opposed a group calling themselves "The Covenant of Zealots" who wanted to fight against the newly formed State of Israel. So he drafted a declaration titled, "*Lo Zu Haderech* (This is Not the Way)," in which he condemned the use of physical force in any act of zealotry. On another occasion, a group of Jews tried to pressure the *Chazon Ish* to issue a statement for their cause but he refused, saying, "Why don't you voice your protest yourselves?"
>
> "Because no one will listen to us!"
>
> "Well, then, why should I listen to you?" he replied.

Good Jews can disagree on when zealousness is appropriate, and when it's not.

King David "shed streams of water because they did not keep the Torah," but he didn't spear Jews to death Pinchas-style. In contrast, when Rav Yehuda heard that a *treif* restaurant opened in Yerushalayim, he complained that "not even a single Pinchas arose from the community!"

Rav Yoshia applies the order *U'shmartem es hamatzo* to both "guarding the *matzos*" and to "guarding [i.e., rushing] to perform mitzvos." The motto: "If a mitzva comes your way, don't let it go sour!"

Zealousness is a character trait. "Only those who are already eager," notes the Talmud, "are urged to become more eager!"

> When Rabbi Yehuda Tzadka used to walk with his children to *shul* he always kept a fast pace and expected them to keep up with him, explaining that it's a mitzva to run to do the service of God ("Let us run to know Hashem!"). In his old age, when he no longer had the strength, Rav Yehuda made a point of always hurrying the last few steps before he entered *shul*.

Yehoshua ben Nun was called a youth even though he was fifty-six years old. The Midrash explains that Yehoshua was quick and agile, and notes that in Hebrew, *na'ar* (youth) is derived from *no'er* (to move, awaken)!

Rabbi Avraham Twerski says this is society's ever-present challenge: to become "zealously" altruistic; or in the inimitable way that the *Chovos Halevavos* always expresses his opinion: "Nothing accomplishes nothing!"

In short: Laziness is a curse — and skill is nil without the will!

> A disciple of the Gerer Rebbe once asked him to recommend a work of *mussar*. The Rebbe replied by pointing to his watch. "This is the greatest source of *mussar*! Every moment wasted is one that will never return!" The Rebbe allotted half an hour twice a day to those who wished to see him and complained bitterly when people were not punctual. "I'm losing minutes!" he would say. "A *zariz* doesn't rush, nor does he arrive early. A *zariz* utilizes every moment and comes right on time…"

The final word goes to Shmuel Ullman: "Years may wrinkle the skin, but to give up enthusiasm wrinkles the soul!"

Moishie is recovering from surgery when a nurse asks him how he is feeling.

"I'm OK, but I didn't like the four-letter word the overzealous doctor used in surgery just as I was nodding off!"

"What did he say?"

"OOPS!"

# Afterword

All of middos can be summarized in one line: have a good name — and a touch of humility!

A good name influences one's entire life, muses Eleazar ben Pedat; it's better than "great riches," says *Mishlei*; and the usually pessimistic *Koheles* adds, "It's even better than "precious ointment."

A name endures, beauty doesn't!

One's reputation in life is critical. It can be easily destroyed when others assume the worst: "As is his name, so is he!"

If you have to choose between your "earned name" and your given name, choose the former, advises Pinchas ben Chama.

People use a derogatory nickname, explains Rabbi Yaakov of Lissa, for those they dislike.

He bases this on the fact that King Saul, who disliked David, referred to him as "the son of Yishai."

It's disrespectful to call people by anything other than their given name ("Do I not have a name?" the Midrash quotes David as asking).

This is why the *Chazon Ish* always advised parents not to choose an unusual name for their children, in order to avoid future embarrassment (*Sefer Chassidim* warns parents not to give their children names of "heathens, idols, nor saints").

When asked by his students to explain his longevity, Reb Yochanan ben Zakkai attributed it to his sensitivity in calling people by their proper names, even if family members used a different name.

"Choose a good name over great riches!" Why? Because, says Eleazar ben Yehuda, "No monument gives such glory as an unsullied name!"

And don't forget the humility!

> One Simchas Torah the *talmidim* of the yeshiva of Slobodka lifted Rav Itzele Peterburger on a chair and enthusiastically sang and danced in front of him. Rev Itzele sang and clapped along.
>
> Later, Rav Isser Zalman Meltzer asked him why, in contrary to his usual humility, he had allowed his students to give him so much *kavod*. Rav Itzele replied, "Humility is a mitzva that is obligatory upon the individual. However, the *talmidim* regard me as a student of Rav Yisroel Salanter and they are fulfilling a great mitzva by paying tribute to me. It would be improper for me to prohibit them from demonstrating this."

In his sefer *Chayei Olam*, the Steipler Rav reminds everyone to recognize their abilities as a gift and a loan from God, gifts that can just as easily be taken away at the first sign of arrogance or conceit.

Because Yosef took no credit for the wisdom of his dream, the Midrash explains he was rewarded with royalty. The Talmud extends this: if the modest are rewarded with greatness then surely the haughty will be crushed!

After Avraham described himself as "dust and ash," God called him "the biggest of giants"!

So who is humble?

One who is aware of his good qualities and prominent stature and yet seeks no credit for them — even in Torah learning.

> Rabbi Eliyahu Chaim Meizel once asked a congregant to arrange a fundraising campaign in Lodz.
>
> "Who am I to stand at the head of such an important project?" the man said.
>
> The *rav* replied, "When a mitzva must be done, there is no place for humility!"

Remember: whenever the Torah talks of helping others, it is repetitive.

For example, *aser te'aser* (give...*ma'aser*), *nason titen* (give [to the poor]), *paso'ach tiftach* (open your hand [to the poor]), etc. The double verb serves a purpose: it reminds that giving consists of "double dipping," in that not only are you helping another but you're helping yourself and building up your own character.

Giving to others is the key to becoming a person with good middos, one whose name is associated with good deeds. When, as Rabbi Yisroel Salanter said, we concern ourselves with *other people's* physical welfare — and with *our own* spiritual welfare — we are on the right path to becoming a true mensch.

# General Endnotes for Further Study

**Introduction**

*Succa* 29a, 42b, 43b; *Vayikra* 26; *Mishnas Rav Aharon* vol. 2; *Shemos* 22:30.

**Week 1**
**On *Ahavas Yisroel***

*Yerushalmi Nedarim* 9; *Vayikra* 19:18; *Avos d'Rabbi Nosson* Chapter 16; *Hilchos Deios*; *Derech Eretz Zuta*, Chapter 2; *Shabbas* 31a; *Nedarim* 40a; *Yoma* 9b.

**Week 2**
**On Aliya**

*Pirkei d'Rabbi Eliezer* 8a; *Bava Basra* 158b; *Bamidbar Rabba* 23:7; *Kesubos* 111a; *Hilchos Melachim* 5:10; *Tehillim* 102:15, 128:5; Klausenberger diary, *parshas Tazria Metzora*, 5748; *Bereishis* 28:11, 16.

**Week 3**
**On Anger, Bearing Grudges**

*Rosh Hashana* 17a; *Yoma* 87a; *Bava Metzia* 58b; *Kiddushin* 40b-41a, 70b; *Kovetz Igros*, letter 154, 157; *Mishlei* 20:3; *Brachos* 29b, 43b; *Ta'anis* 4a; Rashi, *Vayikra* 19:18.

**Week 4**
**On Avoiding Evil People**

*Hilchos Deios* 6:1; *Koheles* 4:9; *Avos* 1:6, 2:9, 5:16; *Makkos* 10a.

**Week 5**
**On Being Concerned for Others**

*Avos* 2:4; *Brachos* 5:1; *Mechilta, Shemos* 13:8; *Bava Basra* 8a; *Zohar, Vayikra* 55a; *Ben Sira* 6:114-15, 9:10, 12:8.

**Week 6**
**On Being Content**

*Tehillim* 91:15; *Yeshayahu* 63:9; *Koheles* 1:7, 8; *Avos* 4:1; *Chachma u'Mussar*, vol. 2; *Eiruvin* 13b; *Nedarim* 81a; *Shemos* 3:11-12.

**Week 7**
**On *Bikur Cholim***

*Sota* 14; *Nedarim* 39, 40a; *Vayikra Rabba* 34; *Shulchan Aruch, Yore Deah* 335:1; *Bereishis* 18; *Ta'anis* 22a.

**Week 8**
**On Borrowing Money**

*Midrash Rabba, Mishpatim* 31; *Yirmiyahu* 15;10; *Sefer Chassidim* #1247; *Shemos Rabba* 31:13; *Yevamos* 122b; *Mishlei* 22:7; *Devarim* 15:1-2: *Shabbas* 63a; *Gittin* 29a; *Koheles* 7:14.

**Week 9**
**On Bribery, Justice**

*Peah* 8:9; *Kesubos* 105a; *Devarim* 16:9; Rema, *Choshen Mishpat* 37; *Vayikra* 19:14; *Shavuos* 3a; *Sanhedrin* 7b, 27b; *Shemos* 23:6, 8; *Sota* 47b.

**Week 10**
**On *Chesed shel Emes*, Eulogies**

*Hilchos Aveil* 14:7; *Mishlei* 17:3, 5; *Avos* 1:3; *Kesubos* 8b; *Brachos* 18a, 62a; *Shulchan Aruch Yore Deah* 344; *Tehillim* 56:9; *Shabbas* 105b, 152a, 153a; *Sanhedrin* 46a.

**Week 11**
**On Clarity in Teaching Torah**

*Hilchos Talmud Torah* 4:4; *Avos* 2:5; *Brachos* 22a; *Eiruvin* 54b; *Sanhedrin* 19b; *Shemos* 12:4, 12; *Devarim* 15:2; *Shemos* 4:8, 7:1-2.

**Week 12**
**On Commerce — Wages and Prices**

*Hilchos Schirus* 13: 6, 7; *Hilchos Shekalim* 4:7; *Kesubos* 105a; *Bava Metzia* 7, 8, 10a, 110b; *Devarim* 24:14-15, 279; *Vayikra* 19:13; *Yoma* 38a; *Bava Basra* 8b-9a; *Succa* 51b; *Bava Kamma* 116b.

**Week 13**
**On Conflict, Controversy**

*Shabbas* 88b, 105b; *Pesachim* 66b; *Sanhedrin* 7a; *Koheles* 7:9, 11:10; *Devarim* 3:26; *Ta'anis* 20b; *Nedarim* 22a, 24a.

**Week 14**
**On *Da'as Torah***

*Chullin* 90b; *Avos* 6; 1; *Shulchan Aruch Yore Deah* 242:2; *Bereishis Rabba* 1:1; *Beitza* 36b; *Rosh Hashana* 25a-b; *Sanhedrin* 87a.

**Week 15**
**On *Derech Eretz*, Respect**

*Avos* 2:2; 3:2; Rav S.R. Hirsch, commentary to *Vayikra* 18:4-5; *Ki Seitzei* 22:10; *Mishpatim* 23:5; *Gittin* 62b; *Brachos* 40a; *Eiruvin* 100b.

### Week 16
### On Doing What's Right — Free Will

*Bava Kamma* 2, 6, 46b; *Pesachim* 25b; *Shemos* 1:4, 9, 12, 15, 18, 21, 23, 31; *Brachos* 34b; *Avos* 3:12, 19; *Devarim* 12:8, 30:19; *Bereishis* 1:2; *Kiddushin* 13b, 58b.

### Week 17
### On Flattery — The "Evil Eye"

*Avos* 2:2, 9, 11; 5:13, 19; *Bava Metzia* 107b; *Pesachim* 50b; *Brachos* 20a, 55b; *Sota* 41b; *Mishlei* 26:28; 28:4, 22,; *Yerushalmi Shabbas* 6:9, 34a; *Tamid* 32b.

### Week 18
### On Fleeing Falsehood — *Emes*

*Pesachim* 113b; *Avos* 1:9; *Sota* 42a; *Bava Metzia* 23b-24a; *Chazon Ish, Emuna u'Bitachon* 4:13; *Tehillim* 119:142; *Sanhedrin* 89b; *Shabbas* 55a, 194a; *Shemos* 23:7; *Vayikra* 19:11; *Yevamos* 65b.

### Week 19
### On Forgiveness

*Tehillim* 145:17; *Sefer Hachinuch* # 241; *Yirmiyahu* 3:12; *Yoma* 23a; *Eiruvin* 13b; *Avos* 2:8; *Bereishis* 18:27; *Yehoshua* 14:15; *Shulchan Aruch, Orach Chayim* 606:1.

### Week 20
### *On Gemilus Chasadim*

*Beitza* 32a, b; *Yevamos* 79a; *Hoshea* 6:6; *Avos* 1:2; *Micha* 6:8; *Bava Metzia* 86b; *Yeshayahu* 66:13; *Ta'anis* 24a; *Pirkei d'Rabbi Eliezer* 12; *Shabbas* 133b; *Devarim* 13:5; *Bereishis* 44:21.

### Week 21
### On Giving the Benefit of the Doubt

*Megilla* 27b; *Avos* 1:6, 2:5, 3:14; *I Shmuel* 25:25; *Mishlei* 22:1; *Yerushalmi Peah* 7:3; *Tehillim* 4:3, 39:9; *Koheles* 7:1, 29; *Brachos* 7b, 17a, 19b; *Shoftim* 6; *Yeshayahu* 6:5; *I Melachim* 19:1.

### Week 22
### Gone Fishing!

Shneur Zalman of Liadi, *Likutei Amarim* 159.

### Week 23
### On Greeting with a Smile

*Avos* 1:15, 4:20; *Sanhedrin* 108b; *Ta'anis* 21a; *Brachos* 17a, 60b; *Kesubos* 111a, b; *Bava Basra* 9b; *Tehillim* 80:8; *Mishlei* 27:19; *Hoshea* 6:6; *Yalkut Shimoni*; *Pirkei d'Rabbi Eliezer* 12.

### Week 24
**On *Hachnasas Kalla*, Sharing in *Simchas***

*Ahavas Chesed* 3:6; *Shabbas* 30b, 130a; *Kesubos* 17a, 62b; *Koheles* 2:2; *Brachos* 6b, 30b-31a; Shach, *Yore Deah* 360:1; *Hilchos Aveil* 14:1; *Megilla* 29a; Rama, *Even Ha'ezer* 65:1; Tur, *Yore Deah* 252, 288, 344.

### Week 25
**On *Hachnasas Orchim***

*Shabbas* 127b; *Ahavas Chesed* 3:1; *Halichos Shlomo* 5; Maharsham, *Orach Chayim* 304-6; Rav Moshe Shternbuch, *Teshuvos v'Hanhagos* 2:197; *Magen Avraham, Orach Chayim* 38:8; *Sefer Chassidim* # 312.

### Week 26
**On Harming Another — Friends and Enemies**

*Sefer Hachinuch* # 338; *Shemos* 2:13; *Tehillim* 24:3, 119:63; *Yalkut Amarim* 2; *Succa* 52a; *Avos* 1:6, 2:9, 4:12; *Ta'anis* 23a; *Shabbas* 106a.

### Week 27
**On Honoring Parents**

*Shemos* 20:12; *Devarim* 5:16; *Kiddushin* 30b, 31a-b, 40a; *Hilchos Mamrim* 6:1; *Megilla* 16b; *Bereishis Rabba* 65; *Mishlei* 1:8; 3:7, 18; 11:4; *Devarim* 22:7; *Bava Basra* 10b; *Sefer Chassidim* #434.

### Week 28
**On Jealousy, Coveting**

*Hilchos Bava Basra* 21a; *Hilchos Deios* 3:1; *Hilchos Teshuva* 5:2; *Zohar, Bereishis* 245a; *Bamidbar Rabba* 18; *Bereishis Rabba* 9:9; *Avos* 4:1, 21; *Hilchos Gezeira* 1:9; *Sanhedrin* 107a; *Kiddushin* 1:9; *Shabbas* 105b; *Nedarim* 9:1.

### Week 29
**On Leadership, Fundraising**

*Yerushalmi Sota* 7:4, 37b; *Avos* 2:12; *Hilchos Matanos Aniyim*, 9:1, 3, 5; *Yerushalmi Shekalim* 3:2; *Bamidbar* 7:12; *Brachos* 55a; *Bereishis Rabba* 7:3.

### Week 30
**On *Loshen Hora*, Slander**

*Shemos* 23:1; *Tehillim* 34:13-14, 75:4, 101:51; *Mishlei* 3:18, 15:4, *Erchin* 16a; *Shulchan Aruch Choshen Mishpat* 420:38; *Vayikra* 19.16; *Erchin* 15b; *Bamidbar Rabba* 19.2; *Brachos* 51b; *Peah* 1:1.

### Week 31
### On Ma'aser

*Sefer Chassidim* #1529; *Gittin* 7b; *Shabbas* 150a; *Kesubos* 50a; *Malachi* 3:10; *Mishlei* 19:17; *Devarim* 15.7; *Kesubos* 68a; *Peah* 4:20.

### Week 32
### On Making Money, Honesty in Business

*Vayikra* 26:3-26; *Avos* 2.5; *Devarim* 28:3-14; *Shemos* 22:24; *Likutei Halachos, Shabbas* 3:3; *Bereishis* 5:22.

### Week 33
### On Making Peace

*Yevamos* 65b; *Yechezkel* 37:26; *Avos* 1:12; *Malachi* 2:7; *Avos d'Rabbi Nosson* 12; *Zohar, Vayikra Rabba* 9:9; *Yalkut Shimoni, Yeshayahu* 32:17, 42:9, 48:22; *Bereishis* 43:23; *Shemos* 4:18.

### Week 34
### On *Midda k'Neged Midda*

*Kiddushin* 30b, 31a, 40a; *II Melachim* 20; *Hilchos Mamrim* 6:1; *Shemos* 23:26; *Megilla* 16b; *Bereishis Rabba* 65; *Chagiga* 4b, 5a; *Mishlei* 3:7, 18, 11:4; *Tosafos, Yevamos* 50a; *Devarim* 22:7; *Erchin* 16b; *Bava Basra* 10b; *II Shmuel* 18; *Sota* 9b; *Sefer Chassidim* #434.

### Week 35
### On Modesty, Humility, Pride

*Sefer Chassidim* #1045; Rabbeinu Yona, *Sha'arei Teshuva* 3:34; *Derech Eretz* 1:27; *Midrash Rabba* 6:6; *Mishlei* 3:18, 34;16:5; 22:4; *Tehillim* 25:9; *Micha* 6:8; *Avos* 4:4; *Mechilta d' Rashbi, Yisro; Sanhedrin* 29a; Eliyahu Hacohen, *Shevet Mussar*, chapter 17; *Avoda Zara* 3:1.

### Week 36
### On Patience, Persistence

*Shabbas* 88b; *Avos* 1:17; *Pe'er Hador*, vol. 4; *Likutei Yehuda, Beshalach; Hilchos Deios* 2:3; *Sefer Chassidim* 30; *Mishlei* 24:16; *Iyov* 14:19.

### Week 37
### On Prayer

*Tehillim* 106:30; *Sanhedrin* 44b; *Shenos Eliyahu, Brachos*, chapter 5; *Tefilla* 6:16; *Shemos Rabba* 21:4; *Zohar, Bereishis* 167b; *Yevamos* 64a, 105b; *Brachos* 4:1, 5:1, 6b, 12b, 13b, 27b, 28b, 30b, 32b; *Ta'anis* 2a, 8a; *Eiruvin* 65a.

### Week 38
### On Rebuke, Offering Advice

*Sanhedrin* 24, 76a; *Bava Basra* 9b, 60b; *Hilchos Rotzeach* 12:14; *Hilchos Deios* 6:7; *Pesachim* 22b, 95; *Bereishis Rabba* 8:8; *Tosafos, Avoda Zara* 1:19; *Vayikra* 19:17; *Koheles* 3; *Yevamos* 65; *Amos* 5:13.

### Week 39
### On Respecting Elders, Honoring *Talmidei Chachamim*

*Makkos* 22b, 24a; *Pesachim* 22b; *Shabbas* 119a; *Sifrei, Devarim* 33;2; *Seder Eliyahu Rabba* 13; *Brachos* 63b, 64a; *Sanhedrin* 24a, 52b; *Avos* 6:1, 6; *Yoma* 28b, 39a; *Kiddushin* 32b, 33a; *Shemos* 3:8, 16; *Midrash Rabba* 11:8; *Bava Metzia* 42a.

### Week 40
### On Selfishness, Sensitivity

*Hilchos Deios* 6:8; *Zohar* 3:85a; *Vayikra* 19:17; *Bava Metzia* 58a, b; *Sota* 8b; *Shabbas* 119b; *Tana d'Bei Eliyahu Zuta* 2; *Bava Kamma* 79b; *Brachos* 6b, 19b; *Devarim* 14:22, 15:8, 10; *Tehillim* 109:31; *Eiruvin* 13b, 16b, 86a.

### Week 41
### On *Shalom Bayis*

*Gittin* 52b; *Avos* 2:15; *Yevamos* 44a, 62b, 65b; *Kiddushin* 31; *Sota* 17a; *Avos d'Rabbi Nosson* 41; *Orach Chayim* 263:3, 606:l; *Hilchos Teshuva* 2:10; *Shabbas* 23b; *Sefer Hachinuch*, 364, 453; *Sanhedrin* 76b; *Bava Metzia* 59a.

### Week 42
### On Shame

Rambam, *Moreh Nevuchim* 1:2; *Brachos* 12b; *Chagiga* 5a; *Bereishis* 2:25, 3:7, 4:1; *II Shmuel* 12:13; *Peah* 1:1; *Bereishis Rabba* 1:4; *Shabbas* 127a.

### Week 43
### On Showing Gratitude, *Hakoras Hatov*

*Bava Kamma* 92b; *Midrash Rabba* 4:2; *Brachos* 7b, 58.

### Week 44
### On Stealing, Returning, Using Lost Objects

*Bava Metzia* 27a, 30b, 31a; *Sha'arei Teshuva* 3:70; *Mishlei* 29:24; *Hilchos Geneiva* 5:11; *Choshen Mishpat* 369; *Gittin* 45a; *Mesillas Yesharim* 11.

### Week 45
### On Supporting Torah Scholars and Institutions

*Mishlei* 3:18; *Sefer Chassidim* #333; *v'Zos Habracha* 33:18; *Shemos* 23:20; *Yeshivas*

*Chachmei Lublin*, vol. 1; Rema, *Yore Deah* 246:1; *Sota* 21a; *Shir Hashirim* 8:7; *Brachos* 64a; *Yeshayahu* 54:13.

## Week 46
### On Taking Advantage of Another Person

*Avos* 6;6; *Kiddushin* 59a; *Kovetz Igros*, letter 89.

## Week 47
### On Teaching Torah to Others

*Sanhedrin* 99a; *Yisro* 20:7; *Tana d'Vei Eliyahu Rabba* 27; *Tehillim* 50:23; *Avos* 2:9; *Magen Avraham, Orach Chayim* 47:1, 50:2.

## Week 48
### On Time Management

*Hoshea* 6:3; *Brachos* 57; *Shabbas* 31b; *Mishna Tamid* 7:4; *Pesachim* 68b; *Sifra, Vayikra* 5:11.

## Week 49
### On Torah as a Protective Umbrella

*Shemos Rabba* 36:3; *Hilchos Yesodei HaTorah* 5:11; *Zohar, Bereishis* 23a, b, 46:28; *Eiruvin* 18b, 54a; *Bava Basra* 7b-8a; *Avos* 2:7; *Vayeira* 18:26; *Sanhedrin* 99a,b; *Megilla* 5a; *Bava Metzia* 60b.

## Week 50
### On *Tzedaka*

*Sefer Chassidim* #144; *Bamidbar* 18:24-28; *Bereishis* 14:18-20, 28:22; *Devarim* 14:28; *Ta'anis* 9a; *Yore Deah* 247, 249:1; *Mishlei* 14:34, 20:7; *Kesubos* 87b; Rambam, *Matanos Aniyim* 7:1.

## Week 51
### On Work

Rashi, *Bava Metzia* 30b; *Shabbas* 150a; *Nedarim* 49b; *Tehillim* 104, 128:2; *Berachos* 8a, 35b; *Avos* 1:10, 2:2, 4:1, 5; *Ta'anis* 25a; *Kiddushin* 29a, 30b; *Sota* 48b; *Yore Deah* 255:1; *Shulchan Aruch Orach Chayim* 156:1; *Pesachim* 113a.

## Week 52
### On Zealousness

*Tehillim* 119:136; *Yoma* 22b-23a; *Vayikra* 6:6, 19:18; *Nedarim* 9:4; *Bamidbar* 25:3, 13; *Hilchos Deios* 7: 7-8; *Kiddushin* 29a; *Makkos* 23a; *Mishlei* 10:4; *Sanhedrin* 9:7, 82a; *Avos* 1:14; *Devarim* 32:35; *Bamidbar* 25:12.

# JOE BOBKER COLLECTION OF BOOKS

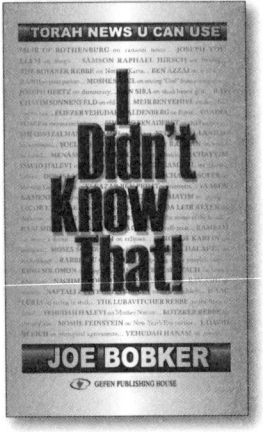

Hardcover • 400 pp
ISBN 978-965-229-398-5
$14.95 • 70 NIS

Hardcover • 312 pp
ISBN 978-965-229-419-7
$18.95 • 80 NIS

Hardcover • 422 pp
ISBN 978-193-014-396-8
$18.95 • 69 NIS

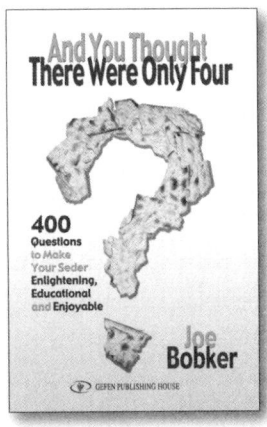

Paperback • 338 pp
ISBN 965-229-366-0
$14.95 • 70 NIS

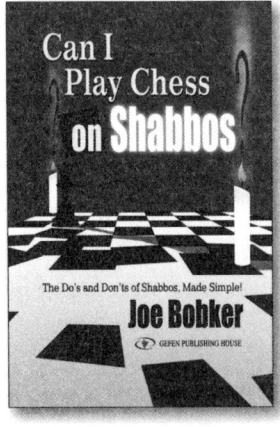

Hardcover
ISBN 978-965-229-422-7
$18.95 • 80 NIS

Hardcover • 280 pp
ISBN 978-965-229-378-7
$18.95 • 80 NIS